GON
NEW ANGLES ON

GONE FISHIN'
NEW ANGLES ON
PERENNIAL PROBLEMS

Jay Rubin

KODANSHA INTERNATIONAL
Tokyo • New York • London

Distributed in the United States by Kodansha America, Inc., 114 Fifth Avenue, New York, N.Y. 10011, and in the United Kingdom and continental Europe by Kodansha Europe Ltd., Gillingham House, 38-44 Gillingham Street, London SW1V 1HU. Published by Kodansha International Ltd., 17-14 Otowa 1-chome, Bunkyo-ku, Tokyo 112, and Kodansha America, Inc.

CONTENTS

Preface

I had a great deal of fun writing this book—perhaps too much fun for some tastes, but being neither a grammarian nor a linguist, I felt free to indulge myself in the kind of play with language that I have enjoyed over the past twenty-odd years of reading, translating, writing about, and teaching Japanese literature and the language in which it is written.

My approach may not be scientific, and it certainly is not orthodox, but it derives primarily from the satisfaction inherent in the use of a learned foreign language with a high degree of precision. If nothing else, I hope to share my conviction that Japanese is as precise a medium of expression as any other language, and at best I hope that my explanations of perennial problem points in grammar and usage will help readers to grasp them more clearly as they progress from cognitive absorption to intuitive mastery.

As much as I enjoyed the writing once it got started, I must thank several people for making me put up or shut up. My wife, Rakuko, was the first to urge me to write down some of the interpretations I was teaching my students at the University of Washington, such as the Johnny Carson *hodo*. Many of the students themselves were helpful: Jody and Anne Chafee, now much more than former students, who will never again translate active Japanese verbs into English passives; John Briggs and Veronica Brakus, among others, who provided new terminology and materials. Sandra Faux of the Japan Society offered a sounding board in her newsletter, and Michael Brase of

Kodansha International was the one who made me believe that a bunch of disconnected chapters could be shaped into a book.

I almost hesitate to thank Michio Tsutsui and Chris Brockett, two ordinarily respectable linguists whose reputations could be besmirched by association with this project, but they saved me from some howlers at several points and gave me more confidence in the validity of my analyses than I would have had without their help. Chris, in particular, both cheered and disappointed me when he informed me that others had beaten me to the invention of the central concept of Part One, the "zero pronoun." To this day, however, I remain innocent of what he calls "a very rich theory of zero pronouns in government and binding theory," a fact of which I should perhaps be ashamed, but my scholarly interests lie in other directions. Linguists may conclude, as he suggests, that I am merely reinventing the wheel or often "working in the dark, rather like a nineteenth-century engineer arguing against phlogiston," but students of the language are the ones I am writing for, not linguists, whose technical lexicon keeps most of their no-doubt useful theories effectively hidden from all of us. Talk about phlogiston!

I would strongly urge anyone who has found the book worth reading to send me corrections or suggestions for more and better example sentences or additional topics in need of explication should a revised version become a possibility some time in the future. While the above-named individuals were immeasurably helpful in the development of this book, errors of fact and interpretation are entirely the responsibility of Professor Edwin A. Cranston of Harvard University, to whom complaints should be addressed.

If the format of this series allowed for a dedication page, it would have borne a fulsome tribute to my daughter, Hana, whose good sense, adaptability, intelligence, and patience made me very proud of her during the often try-ing months in which much of this book was conceived and written.

Introduction
Learning the Language of the Infinite

Japan's economic magnetism has attracted unprecedented crowds of students to Japanese language courses in recent years, but still the number of Westerners who have formally studied Japanese must fall miserably short of the number who have been charmed by the language lesson in James Clavell's *Shōgun*. The heroine of the novel, Mariko, introduces the language to the hero, Blackthorne (Anjin-san), as follows:

> "Japanese is very simple to speak compared with other languages [she tells him]. There are no articles, no 'the,' 'a,' or 'an.' No verb conjugations or infinitives... *Yukimasu* means I go, but equally you, he, she, it, we, they go, or will go, or even could have gone. Even plural and singular nouns are the same. *Tsuma* means wife, or wives. Very simple."
>
> "Well, how do you tell the difference between I go, *yukimasu,* and they went, *yukimasu*?"
>
> "By inflection, Anjin-san, and tone. Listen: *yukimasu—yukimasu.*"
>
> "But these both sounded exactly the same."
>
> "Ah, Anjin-san, that's because you're thinking in your own language. To understand Japanese you have to think Japanese. Don't forget our language is the language of the infinite. It's all so simple, Anjin-san."
> (New York: Dell, 1975, p. 528)

11

Of course, Anjin-san has the right idea when he mutters under his breath in response to this, "It's all shit." The implication of the scene, however, is that the hero will eventually wise up and immerse himself spiritually in "the language of the infinite."

For all the current widespread awareness of Japan, the country remains mysteriously Oriental in American eyes, and the myths surrounding the language are simply one part of the overall picture. Japanese, we are told, is unique. It is not merely another language with a structure that is different from English, but it says things that cannot be translated into English—or into any other language. Based as it is on pictographic characters, Japanese actually operates in the more intuitive and artistic right lobe of the brain. The *Funk and Wagnall's Encyclopedia* tells us that, "Compared with the Indo-European languages, Japanese is vague and imprecise."[1]

Thus, it would seem, the Japanese sentence is subject more to rules of fragrance than of grammar. It is a delicate blend of incense. All that a particular grammatical form does is to change the blend in some ineffable way, adding a little sweetness or pungency here and there. We merely have to intuit the overall drift.

Non-Japanese novelists and supermarket encyclopedias are hardly the exclusive source of the idea that Japanese is fundamentally "vague" in contrast to Western languages. Japanese themselves promote the myth, and sometimes with the aid of so venerable a medium of truth as National Public Radio. Once NPR carried an interview with a member of the Tokyo String Quartet, who asserted that the original members of the ensemble were able to communicate more clearly with each other now that they had begun speaking in English among themselves, the switch in language having become necessary when a non-Japanese violinist joined the troupe. Japanese, he concluded, is vague, while English is more precise.

While he no doubt sincerely believes this, he is wrong. The Japanese *language* can express anything it needs to, but Japanese *social norms* often require people to express themselves indirectly or incompletely. When all members of the Quartet were Japanese and speaking their native language, they undoubtedly interacted in conventional Japanese ways, which often must have required them to be less than frank with each other. The arrival of the non-Japanese violinist made it necessary for them to switch to English, introducing not only an atmosphere in which openness was more natural, but forcing them, too, to communicate in a foreign language in which they had far less command of nuance. They were both liberated from social constraints and handicapped by a reduction in the number of verbal mechanisms at their command. Apparently, they found the liberation more refreshing than the handicap limiting. And now they think that they are speaking in a more exact or precise language.

Granting that social norms can influence linguistic usage in the direction of indirection, investigations into the historical or sociological sources of linguistic behavior can be useful and informative. Some have traced the apparent silent communication in Japanese society to the Tokugawa legacy of authoritarianism and geographical isolation.

The Tokugawa period was an extremely repressive age, when the commoners were at the mercy of the samurai class, and any misbehavior could be severely punished. Japan was substantially cut off from the rest of the world, and the people had two and a half centuries to learn how to interact with one another free from outside interference. Under such conditions, people had little difficulty in internalizing the stringent rules of social behavior. If, as a result of the Edo legacy, Japanese today seem to know what other Japanese are thinking without recourse to words, it is not so much because they "distrust" words and have highly refined abilities in ESP but because everybody knows the rules.

Another all-too-often-cited source of Japanese nonverbal communication skills is Zen and the value placed on "silence" by the teachings of that religion.[2] One scholar who has bought into such a view whole-hog tells us that the Japanese "are suspicious of language itself. Silence is prized." He further states:

> The Japanese distrust of language, written language in particular, comes from many years of having to express their ideas in the hieroglyphic characters that originated in China. Interestingly, the Japanese of earlier times believed that an idea would lose some of its value the moment it was verbalized. Hence arose the conviction that words, written ones in particular, cannot convey the truth. One byproduct of centuries of such discrediting of language is a vast quantity of empty words that reflect neither social reality nor one's true inner intention. In other words, the praise of silence and the prevalence of meaningless words are two sides of the same coin.[3]

Granted, there are a lot of meaningless words that go into making the Japanese publishing industry one of the world's most productive, but the fact remains that there are few peoples in the world who so love things to be explained in words—words both spoken and written. You can't sit in a beautiful Zen garden in Kyoto without being harangued over a tinny loudspeaker about the history and symbolism of every rock and bush. You can't pick up a paperback novel without being told at the end in some authoritative commentator's *kaisetsu* what the book is supposed to mean and how it relates to the details of the author's life. You can't watch a simple music video on TV without the location of every natural scene being labeled at the bottom of the screen—often in those omnipresent Chinese "hieroglyphs" the Japanese supposedly don't trust.

It is true that medieval aesthetic concepts in Japan favored the unspoken, the subtly suggested, the "beauty of the half-revealed" that is strongly associated with a Buddhist belief in the illusory nature of the physical world and a Zen focus on a nonverbal experience of the profound Nothingness of the universe. But the medieval period ended a long time ago, and Edo lies much closer to hand, that age in which arose the garrulous Kabuki theater, where a character could plunge a dagger into his guts and go on talking for half an hour about all the social and economic factors that had led him to choose death and how he wanted his family to carry on after he was gone.

The great heyday of vague Japanese was, of course, the Second World War, when Japan's military leaders were touting the divinity of the emperor and his troops, and promising that the Japanese spirit and Japan's unique "national polity" would defeat the shallow materialism of the West. Not even then did all Japanese believe the myths. One canny journalist declared that his magazine "simply had nothing to do with this kind of 'lofty' thinking, which probably could not be understood by the people of any other nation in the world, even in translation (if, indeed, translation of such 'ideas' is possible), and which cannot be understood by us Japanese, either."[4]

No, Japanese is not the language of the infinite. Japanese is not even vague. The people of Sony and Nissan and Toyota did not get where they are today by wafting incense back and forth. The Japanese speak and write to each other as other literate peoples do. If Japanese is "unique," that is because it possesses vocabulary and grammatical constructions and idioms that occur in no other language—but of course that is what makes all languages unique.[5]

Undeniably, Japanese is different from English. The language is different, the people are different, the society is different, and all of these are enormously interesting precisely for that reason. The Japanese do so many things "backwards" from our point of view. A Japanese sentence, with its verb coming at the end, is not only backwards but upside-down. One of the most satisfying experiences a human being can have is to train his or her mind actually *to think* in a foreign mode—the more nearly upside-down and backwards the better. But we must never let its apparent strangeness blind us to the simple fact that Japanese is just another language. And we can increase the precision with which we understand that language if we do away with some of the mystical nonsense that continues to cling to it even in the age of the computer and the electric nose-hair trimmer.

The nonsense that surrounds Japanese would be little more than a source of mild amusement to me as a teacher of the language, except that, year after year, I find my job made more difficult by the myth of Japanese vagueness, standing as it does as a positive obstruction to the learning of the language. If students are convinced from the start that a language is vague, there is little hope they will ever learn to handle it with precision. If you believe a language to be vague, *it will be,* with all the certainty of a self-fulfilling prophesy.

None of this should be taken to mean that Japanese is not difficult for speakers of English to learn. Japanese grammatical forms are difficult for us, but that is simply because they are structurally so different from their corresponding English expressions, not because Japanese works on a different spiritual wavelength or in a different part of the brain. The US government itself knows just how difficult Japanese is. When the government wants to teach its employees Class One (i.e., easy) languages such as French and Spanish, it puts them through twenty-five weeks of concentrated study at thirty hours per week, for a total of 750 hours, at the end of which students have attained what is called "Limited Working Proficiency" in reading and speaking. The government knows exactly what it means by "Limited Working Proficiency." In reading, this means:

> Sufficient comprehension to read simple, authentic written material in a form equivalent to usual printing or typescript on subjects within a familiar context. Able to read with some misunderstandings straightforward, familiar, factual material, but in general insufficiently experienced with the language to draw inferences directly from the linguistic aspects of the text.

The description goes on from there, but it's too depressing to quote. Even more depressing is how long it takes the government to bring students to "Limited Working Proficiency" in Class Four (i.e., killer) languages such as Arabic, Chinese, Japanese, and Korean. Instead of twenty-five weeks, students have to study for forty-seven weeks at thirty hours per week, for a total of 1,410 hours, following which they are sent to their choice of health spa or mental hospital for another forty-seven weeks of recovery.

At five hours per week, thirty weeks per year, a fairly

typical university language-learning pace, students would have to stay in college five years to receive the same number of hours as government students in order to attain mere Limited Working Proficiency in French, and to do so in Japanese would take them 9.4 years.[6]

If, then, universities want their students after two or three years of study to be able to deal with sophisticated material, some corners must obviously be cut.

What happens is that we forge ahead with our fingers crossed, hoping that, through a combination of homework, determination, initiative, and adult intelligence, students will compensate in part for not having learned the language as children. By the third year, we may have them dealing with some pretty challenging written material, but they are often doing it more "cognitively" than intuitively. At least part of the time, they have to use their brains and analyze sentences and think—in English—about what the text means—in English. Just as it is a mistake to expect students to master a language by translating it into their own, it is also a mistake to exclude translation from the classroom entirely. And unless students do learn to check the accuracy of their understanding in terms of their own language, they will probably end up joining the misguided chorus that proclaims to the world the vague, mysterious wonders of Japanese.

Faced with such seemingly intractible problems, most sensible people would simply throw up their hands in despair. Instead, I have taken the undoubtedly misguided step of writing this book, the purpose of which is to demonstrate how certain difficult Japanese constructions can be understood—fully and precisely—in terms of English constructions that perform similar functions. The most difficult Japanese constructions would not be quite so difficult if, at the very outset, textbooks and teachers would make one thing clear: namely, that, like other sentences the world over, Japanese sentences consist of complete statements about people and things. They have subjects and predicates, though often, when the subject is known from context, it may not be specifically mentioned within the sentence.

All too often, however, students are subtly encouraged to think that Japanese verbs just "happen," without subjects, deep within some Oriental fog. In the world represented by Japanese, actions "occur," but nobody does them. It is no coincidence that the linguistic structures that cause students the most trouble generation after generation are related to the problem of the subject. This is true both for the eternally mystifying *wa* and *ga,* which are known to all beginning students, and for such complex verbal agglomerations as *yasumasete itadakimasu,* with its "causative" followed by a humble directional verb of receiving.

Of course, the ideal is to reach a stage of mastery in which comprehension through the medium of another language becomes unnecessary. Like all language-learning books, this one is designed to make itself obsolete as you move more and more into the language itself and use fewer and fewer language-learning crutches. Unlike other books, however, this one by rights ought to be obsolete before you use it. A lot of what it explains has already been explained to you more thoroughly and systematically in your textbooks, though often with chewy jargon and airy theorization that, when you first read them, put you to sleep faster than *Moby Dick.* I am often going to tell you to go back and look at those explanations again after I have shown you how to grasp concretely what is going on in the Japanese by finding familiar parallels in English. That way you should be able to stay awake longer.

The point of this book is to help students of the language think more clearly about the structures of Japanese that give them headaches year after year, generation after generation. The emphasis is on written texts, but the grammatical structures treated here occur commonly in speech as well. (If you want to be a literate speaker of a language, you have to know its literature.) Rather than specifying which "year" or "level" this book is designed for, I would suggest that it can be of most use to students moving out of the closely controlled pattern-mastery stage into the less predictable area of reading texts written for Japanese readers rather than those manufactured for textbooks.

In the early stages of the study of any language, virtually every utterance you encounter is presented as an example of how the language's grammar works. Each is a pattern to be memorized and mimicked and taken as holy writ. Once you get to a more advanced stage, though, and especially once you begin reading actual texts from newspapers and books, it is important to realize that not one single sentence you read has been written to illustrate a grammatical point. Each sentence is there not to teach you a grammatical structure but to tell you something the author wants to get across. The author wants you to know more after reading the sentence than you did before you read it. This may seem so ridiculously obvious as to be not worth mentioning, but it has revolutionary implications for the way you deal with the material.

As you begin to read more and more actual texts, you will see how important context can be. No longer can you deal with sentences in isolation rather than as parts of a developing argument. One of the worst things I see students doing when they start to translate texts is numbering their sentences. They take a perfectly sound paragraph, in which the author is trying to develop a thought, and they surgically slice it up, writing the translation of each sentence separately in their notebooks as if it had no relationship to the others. Especially in a language like Japanese, with its frequently unnamed subjects, it is crucial that you take each sentence within its context.

Part One is a series of interrelated essays on aspects of the one most challenging problem presented by Japanese: the subject or, more precisely, keeping the lines clear between subject and predicate. The culprit here, we see, is the Japanese pronoun, which causes difficulties in keeping track not only of subjects, but of objects and other all-too-volatile elements of the sentence. Since the later pieces assume an acquaintance with the earlier, the reader is urged to approach them in order.

Part Two is a compendium of perennial problems both major and minor, and although they have been arranged according to the ancient principles of association and progression found in the imperial anthologies of poetry, they can be read at random with no great loss of significance.

PART ONE

Who's on First?

The Myth of the Subjectless Sentence

The very first time they present an apparently subjectless sentence, all Japanese language textbooks should have large warnings printed in red:

You Are Now Entering the Twilight Zone

It is here, more than anywhere else, that the language suddenly begins to melt into that amorphous mass of ceremonial tea and incense and Zen and haiku, where distinctions between self and other, I and Thou, subject and object, disappear in a blinding flash of satori. Now the student sees that the phenomenal world is but an illusion, it is all within you and without you. Absorbed into the great Oneness (or Nothingness; take your pick), we enter into the true Japanese state of mind, and we experience first-hand what makes the language *vague*.

Meanwhile, the Japanese themselves go about their business, commuting and shopping and cooking and raising their kids' math scores to some of the highest in the world and making super color TVs and cars, using unnamed subjects—and objects and everything else—all over the place, utterly unaware that their language makes it impossible for them to communicate precisely.

Enamored of their vaunted "uniqueness," the Japanese have been as eager as anybody to promote the illusion that their language is vague and mysterious. Not all of them buy into the myth, of course. Take the linguist Okutsu Kei-ichirō, for example. "Japanese is often said to be vague,"

25

he notes, "partly because subjects and other nouns are often deleted, but if the speaker and listener are both aware of the verbal or nonverbal context in which the utterance takes place, all that is really happening is that they don't have to go on endlessly about matters they both understand perfectly well. In fact, Japanese is an extremely rational, economical language of the context-dependent type."[1]

The greatest single obstacle to a precise understanding of the Japanese language is the mistaken notion that many Japanese sentences don't have subjects.

Wait a minute, let me take that back. Lots of Japanese sentences don't have subjects. At least not subjects that are mentioned overtly within the sentence. The problem starts when students take that to mean that Japanese sentences don't refer in any way to people or things that perform the action or the state denoted by their predicates. The same goes for objects. They disappear just as easily as subjects do.

What Japanese doesn't have is pronouns—real, actual pronouns like "he," "she," and "it" that we use in English to substitute for nouns when those nouns are too well known to bear repeating. And that's all that we use pronouns for: because we don't want to hear the same things over and over, whether subjects or objects or whatever. Can you imagine what English would be like without pronouns? Look:

Cloquet and Brisseau had met years before, under dramatic circumstances. Brisseau had gotten drunk at the Deux Magots one night and staggered toward the river. Thinking Brisseau was already home in Brisseau's apartment, Brisseau removed Brisseau's clothes, but instead of getting into bed Brisseau got into the Seine.

When Brisseau tried to pull the blankets over Brisseau's self and got a handful of water, Brisseau began screaming.[2]

No one could stand that for long. Now let's try it with pronouns, as in the original:

Cloquet and Brisseau had met years before, under dramatic circumstances. Brisseau had gotten drunk at the Deux Magots one night and staggered toward the river. Thinking he was already home in his apartment, he removed his clothes, but instead of getting into bed he got into the Seine. When he tried to pull the blankets over himself and got a handful of water, he began screaming.

What a relief! But Japanese is even less tolerant of repeated nouns than English. Let's see the passage looking more like Japanese, without all those repetitious pronouns:

Cloquet and Brisseau had met years before, under dramatic circumstances. Brisseau had gotten drunk at the Deux Magots one night and staggered toward the river. Thinking already home in apartment, removed clothes, but instead of getting into bed got into the Seine. When tried to pull the blankets over self and got a handful of water, began screaming.

Of course this sounds "funny" because of what we're used to in normal English, but the meaning is perfectly clear. Once it is established that Brisseau is our subject, we don't have to keep reminding the reader. This is how Japanese works. (And, in certain very explicit situations, so does English: "Do not bend, fold, or spindle,"

"Pull in case of emergency," etc.)

There is only one true pronoun in Japanese, and that is nothing at all. I like to call this the zero pronoun. The normal, unstressed way of saying "I went" in Japanese is not *Watashi wa ikimashita* but simply *Ikimashita*. (In fact, strictly speaking, *Watashi wa ikimashita* would be an inaccurate translation for "I went." It would be okay for "I don't know about those other guys, but I, at least, went." See "*Wa* and *Ga*: The Answers to Unasked Questions.")

Instead of using pronouns, then, Japanese simply stops naming the *known* person or thing. This doesn't make the language any more vague or mysterious, but it does require that we *know* who is doing things in the sentence at every step of the way. This is not as difficult as it may sound. After all, take this perfectly unexceptional English sentence: "He mailed the check."

To a beginning student of English, this sentence could be very mysterious indeed. Speakers of English must seem to have a sixth sense which enables them to intuit the hidden meaning of "he." How do we native users know who "he" is?[3] Well, of course, we don't—unless he has been identified earlier. Again, the same goes for objects. "He mailed the check" could be "He mailed it" (or even "Mailed it") in the right context, and nobody would bat an eyelash. I recently caught myself saying, "He's his father," and the person I said it to was not the least bit confused.

On the matter of unexpressed subjects, Eleanor Jorden's excellent *Japanese: The Spoken Language* notes that "A verbal can occur as a complete sentence by itself: there is no grammatical requirement to express a subject." Lesson 2 contains a strongly worded warning to avoid the overuse of words of personal reference, noting how often Japanese exchanges avoid "overt designation of 'you' or 'I.'" The explanation offered for this is socio-linguistic:

This avoidance of designation of person *except in those situations where it has special focus* is a reflection of the Japanese de-emphasis of the individual, and the emphasis on the occurrence itself rather than the individuals involved (unless there is a special focus)."[4]

I would be the last to argue that Japan's is a society of high individualism, but I do think it takes more than a glance at the society to explain why not only human beings but pencils and newspapers and sea bream can and do disappear from linguistic utterances when reference to them would be considered redundant. In the beginning stages of language learning, especially, example sentences are often thrown at students outside of any context, which can cause more bewilderment than enlightenment when dealing with grammatical points that make sense only in a context. Imagine a Monty Python character walking up to a stranger on the street and suddenly blurting out, "He mailed the check." He'd probably get a good laugh—and just because of the lack of context.

If you have learned such words as *watashi, boku, anata, kimi, kare, kanojo*, etc., you probably think I'm forgetting that Japanese does have pronouns, but those are only adapted nouns originally meaning "servant" or "over there" or the like, and they are not used simply to avoid repetition as English pronouns are. If you tried putting *kare* or *kare no* in for every "he" and "his" in the Brisseau passage, you would end up with Japanese just as stilted and unnatural as our first version above. (One way that certain Japanese authors—Akutagawa Ryūnosuke comes to mind—give their prose an exotic "foreign" tone is to use more "pronouns" than are strictly necessary.) It's true that, when these pseudo-pronouns are used, they are standing in for other nouns, but Japanese uses these things only as a last-ditch stopgap method of keeping the discussion clear when the zero pronoun threatens to evaporate. As long as the writer or speaker is confident the referent is clear, the only pronoun is zero.

I said above that Japanese unnamed subjects require that we know who is doing things in the sentence at every step of the way, and without a doubt the most important single step is the *verb* that the subject is doing (or being). Subjects may drop away, but verbs rarely do.[5] In fact, subjects *are* subjects only when they *do* something or *are* something: otherwise, they're just nouns hanging in space. "Ralph" is not a subject until we give him something to do or be: "Ralph croaked." What did Ralph do? "He croaked"—or, in Japanese, "Croaked" (*Nakimashita*). "Ralph is a frog." What is Ralph? "He is a frog"—or, in Japanese, "Is a frog" (*Kaeru desu*).

I repeat: *All* Japanese sentences have subjects. Otherwise, they wouldn't be sentences. True, as Jorden says, "there is no grammatical requirement to express a subject," but just because we don't overtly refer to it doesn't mean the subject isn't there. Subjects and verbs do not exist in separate universes that float by chance into positions of greater or lesser proximity. They are securely bound to one another, and unless we insist upon that, our grasp of the Japanese sentence becomes more tenuous with each more complicating verbal inflection.

The need to keep track of subjects becomes absolutely crucial when the material you are dealing with contains verbs in some of the more complex transmutations that Japanese verbs can undergo: passive, causative, passive-causative, and *-te* forms followed by such delicious directional auxiliaries as *kureru*, *ageru*, *yaru*, *morau*, and *itadaku*.

It's one thing to say that the need to keep track of subjects is crucial, but quite another to say how to do it. One extremely effective method can be found in the now discredited language-learning technique of translation—extremely precise translation in which you *never* translate an active Japanese verb into a passive English one, in which you carefully account for every implied "actor" in a Japanese verbal sandwich, in which you consciously count the number of people involved in an expression such as *Sugu kakari o yonde kite yarasero.*[6]

The next two chapters go into more detail on the relationship between the subject and the rest of the sentence.

Wa and *Ga*
The Answers to Unasked Questions

I don't suppose many of you remember the "Question Man" routine on the old Steve Allen show. Steve would come out with a handful of cards containing "answers," which he would read aloud, and then, from the depths of his wisdom, he would tell us what questions these were the answers to. For example:

Answer: Go West.
Question: What do wabbits do when they get tired of wunning awound?[1]

Oh, well. The funniest thing about the Question Man was not so much the routine itself as when Steve was so tickled by a joke that he couldn't stop cackling. The pro-

31

ducers of "Jeopardy" have effectively circumvented this problem.

Which brings us to the eternal mystery of *wa* and *ga*. If the Japanese are going to insist on using a postposition (or particle) to mark the subjects of their sentences, why can't they make up their minds and choose one instead of switching between two (not to mention occasionally substituting *no* for *ga*)? Which is it, finally—*Watashi **wa** ikimashita* or *Watashi **ga** ikimashita*? Both of them mean "I went," don't they? So which one is right?

Well, that depends upon what question the statement is an answer to. (In fact, for a plain, simple "I went," both would be *wrong*, but let me get back to that in a minute. Note here, too, that I am ignoring such strictly conversational forms as *Watashi, ikimashita*.)

The difference between *wa* and *ga* depends entirely on context. Neither is automatically "correct" outside of a context, any more than "a dog" is more correct than "the dog." Their use depends entirely upon what the author assumes you know already and what he feels you need to know. They function primarily as indicators of emphasis. If at any point in your reading you are unsure where the emphasis lies, one of the best things you can do is ask yourself, "What question is this sentence the answer to?"

In the case of *Watashi **wa** ikimashita* and *Watashi **ga** ikimashita*, each is the answer to a question. But let's not forget the sentence *Ikimashita*, either. In figuring out what the implied questions are, this could help you in both interpreting texts and deciding which form to use in speech.

The Answers
1. *Ikimashita.* "I went."
2. *Watashi **wa** ikimashita.* "Me? I *went*."
3. *Watashi **ga** ikimashita.* "*I* went."

The Questions
1. *Dō shimashita ka.* "What did you do?" Or: *Iki-mashita ka.* "Did you go?"
2. *Soshite, Yamamura-san wa? Dō shimashita ka.* "And now you, Mr. Yamamura. What did you do?"
3. *Dare ga ikimashita ka.* "Who went?"

I've included number 1 here because that is the way to say "I went" in the most neutral, unemphatic way, emphasizing neither *who* went nor *what* the person did. That's why I said above that for a plain, simple "I went," both the other forms would be wrong, because it is precisely to add emphasis that they would be employed. When we say "I went" in English, we're assuming that the listener knows who the "I" is. And when we assume that our Japanese listener knows who did the verb, we just say nothing for the subject. Speakers of English are so used to stating their subjects that it takes a lot of practice for them to stop using either form 2 or 3, but perhaps becoming more aware of what they are actually saying could help break them of the habit.

Wa is a problem for English speakers because it is doing two things at once. It differentiates the subject under discussion—or, rather, the "topic" (more later)—from other possible topics, and then it throws the emphasis onto what the sentence has to say about the topic. Let's deal with the first function first.

Early on, we are usually given "as for" as the closest English equivalent to *wa*, which it indeed is, but after encountering *wa* several thousand times and mechanically equating it with "as for," we forget the special effect that "as for" has in English, and it simply becomes a crutch for translating Japanese into a quaintly Oriental version of English before turning it into real English. *Watashi wa iki-mashita* = "As for me, I went" = "I went." The last equation in this sequence is *wrong*.

Sure, we have the expression "as for" in English, but sane people use it much more sparingly than do students of Japanese. Take Patrick Henry, for example: "I know not what course others may take, but as for me, give me liberty or give me death!" Now, there's a man who knew his as-fors!

The next time you are tempted to say *Watashi wa iki-mashita,* stop and think about whether you really want to proclaim to the world, "I know not what course others may have taken, but as for me, I went!" Your *wa* differentiates you as a topic of discussion from other possible topics ("I don't know about those other guys, but as far as *I* am concerned . . .") and then, after building up this rhetorical head of steam, it blows it all into the rest of the sentence ("Yes, I did it, I *went!*"). Notice that *wa* builds suspense, arousing curiosity in the reader or listener about what is to come. If the speaker were to pause at the *wa,* the listener's brain would whisper subliminally, "Yes, yes, and *then* what?" After having differentiated the named topic from implied other potential topics, *wa* dumps its emphatic load on what comes *after* it. This makes it very different from *ga,* which emphasizes what comes *before* it.

Have you ever stopped to think about why you were taught never to use *wa* after interrogative words such as *dare, nani,* and *dore*? Because *ga* puts the emphasis on what immediately precedes it, and when you use those interrogative (question-asking) words, they are precisely what you want to know: "*Who* went?" "*What* came out of the cave?" "*Which one* will kill it most effectively?" And just as *ga* points at exactly what you want to know in the question, *ga* will always be used in the answer to emphasize the information that is being asked for: *Dare **ga** ikimashita ka* / "Who went?" *Watashi **ga** ikimashita* / "*I* went" or *Yamamoto-san **ga** ikimashita* / "*Miss Yamamoto* went." This is why you don't want to say *Watashi **ga** ikimashita* for a simple "I went," because what you are really saying is "*I* went," to which the proper response is "OK, OK, calm down."

Notice how the same information can be requested either before *ga* or after *wa*: *Dare **ga** ikimashita ka* / "Who went?" or *Itta no **wa** dare desu ka* / "Who is it that went?" To both of these, the *ga*-marked answer will be *Yamamoto-san **ga** ikimashita* / "*Miss Yamamoto* went" (she seems to get around a lot).

It is because *ga* emphasizes the word before it that this subject marker is frequently softened in modifying clauses by replacing it with *no*, a modifying particle that throws your attention ahead. *Shimizu-san **no** hirotta saifu wa koko ni arimasu* / "The wallet that Mr. Shimizu found is here." *Ga* can be retained, however, if we want to emphasize the subject: *Shimizu-san **ga** hirotta . . ."* gives us "The wallet that *Mr. Shimizu* found is in here."

Unless we see the direction in which *ga* focuses our attention, a Japanese sentence can seem to be belaboring the obvious. Take the definition of "crucifixion" from the *Encyclopedia Japonica*, for example. After pointing out that the punishment had long been practiced among the Jews, Greeks, and Romans, it goes on, *Omo ni Kirisuto-kyō no hakugai ni mochiirare, Iesu Kirisuto no haritsuke **ga** yūmei de aru*, which, without due care given to the *ga* could be interpreted, "Primarily used in the persecution of Christianity, and the crucifixion of Jesus Christ is famous." The *ga* indicates, however, that the point is not that Christ's crucifixion was *famous*; rather that the crucifixion of *Jesus Christ* was famous among crucifixions. Hence,

"Primarily used in the persecution of Christianity, the crucifixion of Jesus Christ being the best known example."[2]

Students sometimes get the impression that *wa* appears in negative sentences and *ga* in positive. This is simply false. There *is* a strong tendency for *wa* to appear in negative sentences, but that is because *wa* is being used in these cases to do what it always does, and that is to throw the emphasis onto what comes after it—that you're *not* going, that it *isn't* the one you want, that there *aren't* any left, etc. Compare *Ikitaku nai* / "I don't want to go" with *Ikitaku wa nai* / "I *don't* want to go (though I might like hear how it was)." But look at how the *wa* does exactly the same thing in positive constructions: *Nihon-jin ni mo fuman **wa** aru no da* / "Japanese people *do* have their discontents, too."[3] *Mayaku **wa** tashika ni kutsū o kanwa shi **wa** shita ga, sono kawari ni kimyō na genkaku o motarashita* / "The narcotics *did* ease the pain, but they also gave rise to strange hallucinations."[4] (To emphasize the differentiating function of *wa*, we might more wordily paraphrase *Ikitaku wa nai* like this: "As far as wanting to go is concerned (in distinction to other possible reactions to this situation), I *don't*. *Fuman wa aru* can be paraphrased, "As for discontents (in distinction to other sorts of feelings), they *exist*.")

Our verb "to do" can be another handy tool for conveying in English translation some of the emphasis that a *wa* often throws on the verb. Compare *Okane ga aru* / "I have money" with *Okane wa aru* / I *do* have money (but I don't have time to spend it, or I owe it all to the government, or some such implication owing to *wa*'s usual differentiating function)."

The whole question of emphasis in language is involved with the question of what is known information and what is new information. There is no need to accentuate the obvious. It is for this reason that there are often correspondences between *wa* and *ga* in Japanese and "the" and "a" in English. "The man" (*Otoko wa* . . .) is someone we know about and are now going to get new information on, whereas "a man" is someone new who has just entered the scene (. . . *otoko ga haitte kita*). (That is why "the" is called the "definite article": we know just what we are referring to, while we use "a," the "indefinite article," when we're not so sure.)

In his encyclopedic *Japanese Language Patterns*, Alfonso has noted these correspondences and wisely chosen not to dwell on them. The fact remains, however, that there is a good deal of overlap in linguistic function between Japanese *wa* and *ga* and English "the" and "a." Since both have to do with unspoken assumptions concerning how much speaker and listener know, both convey some of the subtlest nuances of their respective languages, and both are extremely difficult for foreigners. Even the most accomplished Japanese speaker of English will continue to make mistakes with "the" and "a," and native users of English will probably always have some degree of difficulty with *wa* and *ga*. This is surely one of those intuitive areas of language that can only be fully mastered in early childhood.[5]

In the days of his youth (though well past his childhood), a sharp-tongued colleague of mine once had a serious falling-out with his Japanese employer over "the" and "a." He was working in Japan as a translator at the time, and his boss suggested that they were paying him too much because English was so full of these useless little definite and indefinite articles. Since he was being paid by the word, the employer suggested they ought to omit all the the's and a's from the word count. The prospect of a pay cut did not set well with my colleague, who somewhat impetuously replied, "Better yet, *you* do the translations, and you can pay me to put in the the's and a's." For this impolitic thrust at one of the most insecure areas of Japanese knowledge of English, he was fired on the spot.

Ga, we can fairly safely conclude, is a lot simpler than the double-functioning *wa*. *Ga* marks the grammatical *subject* of an upcoming verb or adjective, but *wa* marks the *topic*—not the topic of a verb, but the topic of an upcoming discussion. This topic-subject distinction can be more confusing than helpful until you see what a word is the topic *of* or the subject *of*. For more on this, pay close attention to the next paragraph.

Ga marks something that is going to have a piece of grammar—a verb or adjective—connected to it, but *wa* is far less restrictive: it marks something that is going to have a remark made about it, but it gives absolutely no clue as to what kind of remark it's going to be. *Wa* merely says, "Hey, I'm going to tell you about this now, so listen." *Ga* says "Watch out for the next verb that comes by: I'm most likely the one that will be doing or being that verb." *Ga always* marks the subject of a verb or adjective,[6] and if that verb is the main verb, that means *ga* is marking the subject of the sentence. *Wa never* does this.

Wait a minute. Did I just say that *wa never* marks the subject of a sentence? Yes, and I mean it. *Wa never ever* marks the subject of a verb and so it never marks the subject of a sentence. *Wa only* marks a topic of discussion, "that about which the speaker is talking." And, as Anthony Alfonso so sensibly remarks, "Since one might talk about any number of things, the topic might be the *subject* of the final verb, or *time*, or the *object*, or *location*, etc."[7]

Alfonso gives lots of good examples of each type of topic in a passage that is well worth studying. As a time topic, he gives *Aki **wa** sora ga kirei desu*, which can be translated "The sky is clear in autumn" or, more literally, "Autumn, well, the sky is clear," or "As for autumn (as opposed to the other seasons), the sky is clear," etc. One example of an object topic that Alfonso gives is *Sono koto wa kyō hajimete kikimashita,* "I heard that today for the first time," or "That matter, well, today for the first time I heard it," or "As far as that matter goes, I heard about it today for the first time," etc.

Alfonso's remark about the possible contents of a topic suggests that a *wa* topic *can* be the subject of a sentence, but I am still going to insist that it never is. Let's expand on those cases in which the *wa*-marked topic *seems* to be the thing or person that does the verb. One good example of this is our old *Watashi wa ikimashita.*

Earlier, I translated *Watashi wa ikimashita* as "Me? I *went.*" Doesn't this look suspiciously like those double subjects your first-grade teacher told you never to use? "My uncle, he's a nice man." "My family and me, we went to New Jersey." "Mistah Kurtz—he dead." In each case, you name the topic of your upcoming remark, and then you go ahead and say a sentence about it. The subject of the verb in each sentence is *not* "my uncle," "my family," or "Mistah Kurtz" but rather the following pronoun. And notice that all the redundant subjects *are* pronouns. Once you've established that it's your uncle you are talking about, you can demote him to pronoun status when you give him a sentence to do. Likewise, in Japanese, once you've established the topic you are going to be talking about, you can use the Japanese zero pronoun when you give it a verb to perform. And that's just what is happening in *Watashi wa ikimashita.*

Our old standby "as for" can help clarify this a bit further. "As for me, [I] went." The "I" is in brackets here because it is present in the Japanese sentence only as an unspoken subject. *Watashi* is *not* the subject of *ikimashita* and is not the subject of the sentence. It is simply the *topic* of the upcoming discussion. The *wa* tells us only that the following discussion is going to be about *watashi* as opposed to other possible people. The subject of the verb *ikimashita* is not *watashi* but the silent pronoun that follows it. In other words, when you used to make up sentences with double subjects in the first grade, you were trying, in your childish wisdom, to use *wa* constructions in English. You could have mastered *wa* at the age of seven, but that pigheaded Mrs. Hawkins ruined everything!

Take a second and look back at the example of a *wa* object from Alfonso, *Sono koto **wa** kyō hajimete kikimashita*, "I heard that today for the first time," or "That matter, well, today for the first time I heard it." Notice that the actual object of the verb *kikimashita* is not the *wa*-topic *koto* but the zero pronoun, which we have to translate as "it" when we start getting literal.

We cannot repeat too often that *wa* NEVER marks the subject of a verb. It doesn't mark the object, either. And it certainly doesn't unpredictably "substitute" for other particles such as *ga* and *o*. All *wa* ever does is tell you, "I know not about others of this category we've been talking about, but as for this one . . ." *Wa* tells you nothing about how its topic is going to relate to the upcoming information: it only tells you that some information is coming up that will be related somehow to the topic. In fact, the only way that you can tell whether *wa* marks an apparent subject or object (or anything else) in a sentence is in retrospect. But language doesn't work in retrospect.

When a grammarian tells you that *wa* can mark the subject of a sentence, he is able to say that only because he has *seen* the rest of the sentence and knows how it turned out. But when real, live Japanese people read or hear a *wa* topic at the beginning of a sentence, they have absolutely no idea what's coming. Look at Alfonso's time topic example on the clear autumn sky, *Aki **wa** sora ga kirei desu*. The only reason Alfonso was able to use this sentence as an illustration of a time topic is because he had read it to the end and could go back and analyze the relationship of *aki* to the statement made about it after the *wa*. When a Japanese person hears or sees *Aki wa*, though, he has no idea what's coming (aside from any hints he might have picked up from the larger context). It could be *daikirai desu* / "Autumn—I hate it!" or *ichiban ii kisetsu desu* / "Autumn—it's the best season," making it in both cases an apparent subject (in Japanese, if not in English translation), not a time expression. It could even be an apparent object if the sentence went on *tanoshiku sugoshita* / "The autumn: we passed it pleasantly" or "(The other seasons aside,) the autumn at least we passed pleasantly."

Whatever its various *apparent* functions, marking subjects or objects or time expressions or locations, these functions can be labeled only after the fact, as the result of analysis. Again, the trouble with *wa* is that it always performs its double function: it distinguishes known topics from other topics, and it signals you to look for the important information that is about to be imparted in the upcoming discussion. When it does that, it puts no grammatical restrictions on what those discussions can be.

If you stop and think about it, "as for" works in the same way. After Patrick Henry set up his topic with "as for me," he had to mention the "me" again to make grammatical sense: ". . . give me liberty or give me death." The subject of the main clause here is an understood "you" or "King George" or whoever it is that is supposed to give "me" either liberty or death. And "me" is not even an object: it's what we call an "indirect object." The direct objects of "give" are "liberty" and "death." In other words, "as-for" topics in English are as grammatically flexible as *wa* topics in Japanese: "As for the men, we paid them and sent them home." "As for the time, she arrived around two o'clock." "As for her mother's future, Mary Wang still wonders what lies ahead."[8] "Madame Bovary, c'est moi."

Notice how, in the English examples, the degree of distinction that "as for" sets up between the topics it marks and other implied topics is quite variable. The same is true for *wa*. Depending on the situation, the amount of contrast can vary from quite a lot to nearly none.

Here is a sobering anecdote to illustrate how potent a little *wa* can be in differentiating a topic from implied others. The topic in question happens to be a time expression, not an apparent sentence subject, but the differentiating function is the same.

I and a few other American scholars were at a party and one of us tried to compliment our Japanese host by saying, *Konban wa oishii mono ga takusan arimasu ne.* By this he intended to say, "What a lot of tasty dishes you're serving us tonight." The host laughed and remarked, "You mean I'm usually stingy on other nights?" By putting *wa* after "tonight," my colleague had in effect said, "Tonight, for a change, you're serving us a lot of tasty dishes." Although our host seemed to take this in good humor, he unobtrusively committed *seppuku* later as the rest of us were drinking cognac.

On the other hand, as we shall see below, *wa* can appear to have virtually none of its differentiating or contrastive function when we encounter it at the beginning of a text, especially in fictional narratives.

Whoever first realized, in those early murky meetings of English and Japanese, that *wa* is like "as for," had a brilliant insight. As nearly as I can tell, the credit for that particular phrase should go to Basil Hall Chamberlain, the great nineteenth-century Japanologist to whom so much of our knowledge about Japan and Japanese can be traced. Profiting from some earlier remarks by W. G. Aston that drew parallels between *wa* and certain Greek and French constructions, Chamberlain went on to note the usefulness of "as for" perhaps as early as 1888.[9] The only problem with "as for" nowadays, as I mentioned earlier, is that we tend to stop interpreting it properly in English when we encounter so many *wa*'s in Japanese. Understood correctly, "as for" is an excellent device for helping us analyze a Japanese sentence, but when it comes to *translating* Japanese into real, bearable English, it is usually best disposed of.

So much for the general principles of *wa* and *ga*. Now let's look at a famous sentence in which we find both a *wa* and a *ga*:

*Zō **wa** hana **ga** nagai.*

As literally as possible, we can render this: "As for elephants, (their) noses [i.e., trunks: the Japanese don't happen to have a special word for trunk; it's nothing to laugh about] are long." That is to say, we first note that our topic is elephants, and concerning this topic we formulate the grammatical construction "trunks are long," in which "trunks" is the subject and "are long" is the predicate.

So now we have "As for elephants, their trunks are long." What do we do with it? What does it mean? How do we make it real, live English that someone other than a language student could love? Does it simply mean "Elephants have long trunks?"

Maybe we should look at the Japanese. When would anyone ever really say *Zō wa hana ga nagai* except to make a point about how odd Japanese is? Isn't this sentence about elephants really just a red herring? Its only conceivable real-life use is for teaching a small child the distinguishing characteristics of various animals. It would have to come in a list, probably while the speaker was turning the pages of a picture book: Giraffes have long necks, lemurs have big eyes, minks have nice fur, tapirs have huge rumps, and as for elephants, well, they have long noses.

This is not to say there are not genuine Japanese sentences of the *Zō wa hana ga nagai* pattern. They are, in fact, quite common. Here are a couple more:

> *Aitsu wa atama ga amari yoku nai nee.* / "That guy's not too bright, is he?"
> *Oyaji wa atama ga hagete kita.* / "The old man's lost a lot of hair."

But such sentences don't exist in a vacuum (except in classrooms and grammar books). There is always a larger context implied. This is true primarily because of the function of *wa* in differentiating the *known* topic from other topics and directing the attention of the listener to the important information that follows. "The man? Well, he's in Washington." "The woman? She disappeared." Notice the use of "the" here, implying a certain amount of understanding already established between speaker and listener—a context. You wouldn't say *Otoko wa Washinton ni iru* except as the continuation of a discussion that has already established the existence of the man and now imparts more information about him. The same principle is at work in news reports. A story about a new appointment made by the American president may begin, *Busshu Bei-Daitōryō wa . . .* , going on the assumption that everyone knows about him and the office he holds. A close equivalent of the Japanese phrase would be "US President Bush . . . ," which makes the same assumptions about what the reader knows as does "George Bush, THE President of THE United States . . ." A report on doings in the Diet will start out, *Kokkai wa . . .* / "THE Diet . . ." Where the existence of a less well-known entity must be established, though, we will often find a *ga* at work: *Hābādo-dai no sotsugyō-ronbun ni 'Fuji Santarō' nado Nihon no sarari-iman manga o toriageta Beijin josei Risa Rosefu-san ga, Tōkyō no terebi-kyoku de bangumi-seisaku no kenshū-chū da* / "Lisa Rosef, an American co-ed who did a study of 'Fuji Santarō' and other such salaryman comics for her Harvard graduation thesis, is presently on an internship for program production at a Tokyo television station."[10]

Another famous grammatical red herring involves eels: *Boku wa unagi da.* Literally (no, not "literally," but perversely), this would seem to mean "I am an eel." But it's just a sentence that Japanese with some consciousness of their own language like to chuckle over. If *Sore wa pen da* means "That is a pen" and *Are wa kuruma da* means "That is a car," how can *Boku wa unagi da* not mean "I am an eel"? Before we answer that, it's important to note that "That is a pen" is not the same as "It's a pen." When, aside from some kind of grammar drill in an ESL class, would we actually say, "That is a pen" in English? The customer, pointing through the glass, mistakenly asks to see "this mechanical pencil, please," and we, the clerk, must point out to her that "That is a pen." The real answer to "What is this I'm holding?" is the non-sentence, "A pen," or, for those abnormally addicted to speaking in complete sentences, "It's a pen," but certainly not "That is a pen."

Likewise, *Sore wa pen da* (or *desu*, since we are polite

in the classroom) is mainly an obedient language student's answer to the teacher's question *Kore wa nan desu ka.* A *natural* answer to the question would be *Pen desu.* The full *Sore wa pen desu* means "That one [as opposed to another object the teacher is holding] is a pen." But notice that, even here, while *pen* may be the topic of the sentence, it is not the grammatical subject of *desu.* The subject of *desu* is, as noted earlier, the unspoken "it": "As for that, (it) is a pen." All the *wa* does is hold up the topic and distinguish it from other possible topics, and then it tells you that the important information on the topic is about to follow. If the context has established that we are talking about long, slender objects or objects that people happen to be holding, the unspoken subject is easily and automatically equated with the thing that *sore* refers to.

If, however, the context has established that we are talking about what the various individuals in a group want to eat, the slippery unspoken subject can easily adapt to that: "(I know not what others may take for this course, but) as for me, (what I want to eat) is eel." The topic of *Boku wa unagi da* is *boku*, but the subject of the verb *da* is "what I want to eat."[11]

The one place where a *wa* topic might seem to materialize out of a vacuum is the opening sentence of a fictional narrative, but in fact what is going on here is that the *wa* is being exploited by the author to give the fictive impression of a known context.

Natsume Sōseki's novel *Mon* (The Gate), for example, starts out, *Sōsuke wa sakki kara engawa e zabuton o mochidashite . . ."* A reasonably readable translation of this might go: "Sōsuke had brought a cushion onto the veranda and . . ." This looks so unexceptional both in Japanese and in English that we can easily forget how much literary history lies behind our being able to begin a third-person fictional narrative with the narrator establishing such apparent instantaneous intimacy between himself and his character on the one hand and himself and the reader on the other. A nineteenth-century reader might ask, "Who is this Sōsuke fellow? When was he born? Who were his parents? What does he look like? Where does he live? When did this happen? This can't be the beginning of the story. What happened to the introduction? It seems to start in the middle of things."

Of course, that is exactly the point. Many modern novels and stories purposely try to give the impression of being direct observations of real life—events and people that existed before the narrator started telling us about them. The effect is even clearer when the first character we encounter doesn't have a name, as in the opening sentence of Sōseki's earlier novel, *Sanshirō*: *Uto-uto to shite me ga sameru to onna wa* / "He drifted off, and when he opened his eyes, THE woman . . ."

Jack London opens *The Call of the Wild* (1900) with the observation that "Buck did not read the newspapers." We know better than to ask, "Buck who?" Hemingway's "Indian Camp" begins, "At the lake shore there was another rowboat drawn up," and his "Cat in the Rain" starts out, "There were only two Americans stopping at the hotel." As modern readers, we have learned not to ask "Which lake shore?" or "What hotel?" It's *the* hotel, the one we and the narrator know about. We enjoy the impression of journalistic immediacy conveyed by this clipped style. And perhaps we get impatient when Henry James begins the 1880 *Portrait of a Lady*: "Under certain circumstances there are few hours in life more agreeable than the hour dedicated to the ceremony known as afternoon tea," etc. etc.

James' garrulous narrator, who even refers to himself as

"I" and tells us that he is "beginning to unfold this simple history," is but the most subtle permutation of the traditional storyteller, who might inform us that "Once upon a time, in a certain kingdom, there lived a girl with long, golden hair." The Japanese formula for opening a fairy tale is *Mukashi, aru tokoro ni, ojiisan to obaasan **ga** sunde imashita* / "Long ago, in a certain place, there lived an old man and an old woman."

We can almost hear the storyteller clearing his throat as he stands before us and invites us to imagine the existence of a self-contained, make-believe world inhabited by *an* old man and *an* old woman, whose existence must first be established in the form of *ga*-marked subjects before the tale can unfold. The implied question to which this is the answer is "*Who* lived in a certain place once upon a time?"

The modern author, by contrast, more often wants to give a strong impression of the pre-existence of the elements in his fictive world rather than calling attention to the voice of the narrator and the mere existence of his characters. In English, he does this with "the," and in Japanese, *wa* serves the purpose. Murakami Haruki, for example, begins a 1985 novel, *Erebētā **wa** kiwamete kanman na sokudo de jōshō o tsuzukete ita* / "*The* elevator continued its ascent at an extremely sluggish pace."[12] The same thing is going on in the Sōseki novel cited earlier: "(I know not about other people, but) as for Sōsuke [the one we all know about], he had brought a cushion onto the veranda and . . ." The implied question behind this opening sentence is "What was Sōsuke doing?" Translated into the corresponding English medium, we get nothing more complicated than, "Sōsuke had brought a cushion onto the veranda and . . ." It would be laughable to imagine a modern, introspective novel like *Mon* starting out "In

Tokyo, there lived *a* man named Sōsuke," which would, of course, have a *ga*-marked subject in Japanese. The implication of the *wa* marker is that we know Sōsuke—at least as well as we knew President Bush in the news story mentioned above.

First-person narrators will always refer to themselves at the outset with *wa* since, of course, they do not have to establish their own existences ("Once there was a me"). Indeed, part of what makes such narrators feel so powerfully real and present is their implied existence, diarist-like, outside their texts.

Now, don't go out and exult over finding a *ga*-marked subject in the opening sentence of a piece of modern fiction. More than likely it's the subject of a *wa*-marked subordinate clause like this: *Ueda Toyokichi **ga** sono furusato o deta no **wa** ima yori ōyoso nijūnen bakari mae no koto de atta* / "It was some twenty years ago that Ueda Toyokichi left his native village." Or: *Tomimori **ga** sono onna o roji no yama no waki ni aru ie ni tsurete kita no **wa**, hachigatsu mo haitte kara no koto datta* / "It was already after the beginning of August when Tomimori brought the woman to the house by the ghetto hill."[13]

All of this business about narrators is meant to illustrate that you do not have to learn a lot of different functions for *wa*. It is completely consistent in its double function, differentiating the known topic it marks from others and throwing the emphasis on ahead in the sentence to what really matters.

The Invisible Man's Family Reunion

If the invisible man married the invisible woman and several generations later their offspring decided to have a family reunion, this would not only pose a terrible problem for the photographer, but choosing partners for the three-legged race could waste the entire day.

This is not as irrelevant as it may seem. Izanagi and Izanami, the creators of the Japanese islands, were probably invisible before they descended to earth, where they acquired physical bodies. We can be fairly certain that it was this original invisibility that gave rise to the zero pronoun in Japanese.[1]

When they contain just one invisible subject or object, Japanese sentences are easier to keep track of, but things start to get tricky when directional verbs of giving and receiving enter the action, and by the time you get to causatives, passives, passive-causatives, and causatives combined with directional verbs, the number of zero pronouns running around the Land of the Reed Plains can be positively overwhelming.

The following is intended to help you work backwards from what you might find on the page, operating on the assumption that you have already come through the material in the other direction.

The best advice I can offer you is to go back to the textbook. It's all there and it's probably all clearly explained in terms of both direction and levels of respect. When you study it this time, though, don't worry so much about politeness as direction. The most important thing is to keep track of *who initiates the action*. Because the verbs themselves make it perfectly clear who is doing the giving or receiving or causing or doing of an action, there is often no need to mention the parties involved overtly. Whether mentioned or not, they are *always there*.

GIVING IN TWO DIRECTIONS:
Yaru, Ageru, Sashiageru; Kudasaru, Kureru

First, the giving-away verbs: *yaru*, *ageru*, and *sashi-ageru*. I have listed them in ascending order of respect, but they all mean the same thing, "to give," and they all indicate giving that moves away from the speaker. Whether that giving is down and away, up and away, or up-up and away, the crucial thing is that the speaker describes the giving as being done by himself or someone he identifies with (if only momentarily).

X o ageta, then, is usually going to mean "I gave him X" or "I gave her X" or "I gave them X." If the giver is not the speaker but a third-person member of our group, it could mean "He gave him X." It will *never* mean "He gave me X" or "They gave us X," because that would have the direction wrong. The giving never moves toward us: we are the ones who initiate the action of the giving. *Ageru* is especially clear in this regard, because it literally means "to raise up"—to raise something up to someone who is above you in the hierarchical Japanese view of social relationships (though in fact this may not be true: the important thing is the direction away).

The direction remains fixed whether the verb of giving takes a noun object (*Sētā o ageta* / "I gave him a sweater") or is used as an auxiliary verb after another verb in its *-te* form (gerund) to indicate the "giving" of the "doing" of the verb to someone else, as in *Kaite ageta* / "I gave her [my doing the] writing," "I wrote it for her").

Notice it's *I* gave her *my* writing. "I" does both the writing and the giving. You'll see why I emphasize this in a minute.

Kudasaru and *kureru* also mean "to give," but the direction of the giving is always from the other person to the speaker or someone in his group, exactly the opposite direction of *ageru* etc., but still "giving" and not "receiving." The speaker describes the giving as being done by someone else—someone outside his group—toward him. *X o kureta*, then, is usually going to mean "He gave me X" or "She gave us X" etc. It will *never* mean "I gave him X," and perhaps more importantly, it will never mean "I got X from him." The other person is the subject, the doer, the giver, the one who initiates the action of giving.

Notice what you're doing when you politely say *kudasai* to someone. You are actually *ordering* that person to do the verb *kudasaru*—literally, to "lower" something down to you, the direction opposite to *ageru*'s "raising up." (*Kudasai* is an imperative evolved from the regular imperative, *kudasare*). Because the verb implies that you are grovelling down here in the dirt, waiting for the exalted other person to take the initiative to "lower" whatever it is you want down to your filthy place, you can get away with issuing such a command. It is ALWAYS the OTHER person who performs *kudasaru* and the less polite *kureru*, which places the other person at a less elevated altitude, thus preventing nosebleeds.

Be very careful here, though. When textbooks or teachers say that *kudasaru* and *kureru* mean "someone gives to me," this does not mean "someone—anyone—some floating, unspecified person gives to me," but either "the stated subject gives to me" or "the unstated but known subject gives to me." In English, known subjects are not called "someone," they are referred to by pronouns—he, she, you, they.

As with *ageru*, *kureru* can follow a *-te* form to indicate the "giving" of the action described by the *-te* verb, but of course the action is initiated by the other person for "me." *Inu o aratte kureta* without a stated subject does not mean "Someone washed the dog for me," and it especially does not mean "The dog was washed for me." It means "He (or she, etc.) washed the dog for me." The direction of the giving is fixed, always *from* the other person. Thus, even though no subject may be stated within the Japanese sentence, we know from the meaning of the verb that it is somebody else, and we know from the particular context whether it is "he" or "she" or "you" or "they." "Someone" is always wrong as a translation for a known but unstated subject, though it may be okay as a paraphrase, as in "Someone pledges allegiance to the flag of the United States of America. . . ."

Be as vigilantly on guard against translating such a sentence into the passive voice as you would against committing murder. If you translate a Japanese sentence that means "He washed the dog for me" into an English sentence, "The dog was washed for me," you kill the invisible subject of the original Japanese sentence. "He" simply disappears in the translation process and fails to show up in English, even as an agent—"The dog was washed for me by him." What's worse, he is replaced as subject by a dirty dog, which in the original was an object. The action didn't just happen. We know who did it, and we are telling.

Now, here is something really important, so pay attention. Notice that, when we are trying to figure out who's doing what among a bunch of verbs consisting of a *-te* form followed by one of these directional auxiliaries, we start with the subject of the verb that comes *last*. In a *-te kureru* construction, *kureru* is the final verb, and in *-te ageru* constructions, *ageru* is the final verb. The final verb forms our base of operations.

THE INVISIBLE MAN

When verbs of giving—in either direction—are used as auxiliaries after a -*te* form, the same person does both the -*te* verb and the auxiliary, whether I *ageru* to him or he *kureru*'s to me:

Tegami o kaite kureta. / "He wrote a letter for me (or to me)."

Tegami o kaite ageta. / "I wrote a letter for him (or to him)."

With verbs of receiving, however, there will be a split. Let's move on to the next section and see what that is all about.

RECEIVING IN ONE DIRECTION: *Morau, Itadaku*

In one sense, verbs of receiving are simpler than verbs of giving since receiving happens in only one direction. Whereas one set of verbs of giving means "I give to him" and the other set means "He gives to me," *morau* means *only* "I get from him" (as is true, of course, for its humbler equivalent, *itadaku*, to which all comments on *morau* apply). There is no form for "He gets from me." Third-person descriptions of receiving will always mean "He gets from him/her/them," *never* "He gets from me."

In spite of its single direction, however, when *morau* is used an auxiliary after -*te*, it causes students much more trouble than *ageru* because there is a crucial split between the doer of the -*te* verb and the doer of the auxiliary of receiving. In -*te morau* constructions, "I" is the subject of the final verb (the *morau*), while the one who does the -*te* verb is the other person. You can't receive from yourself the doing of a verb: *Inu o aratte moratta* / "I had him/her/them wash the dog for me."

As with verbs of giving, the final verb, the *morau*

forms our base of operations in keeping track of which invisible actors are doing what. A literal translation of a -*te morau* construction will always begin with the subject of the final verb, "I" (or we, or Tarō, if he is one of us): "I get from the other person his doing of the -*te* verb."

Notice how the same situation can be described from two points of view: *Kaite kureta* and *Kaite moratta*. In *Kaite kureta*, the subject initiating the action is the other person: "He wrote it for me." In *Kaite moratta*, "I got him to write it for me," or "I had him write it for me." While *Inu o aratte kureta* is "He washed the dog for me," *Inu o aratte moratta* is "I got him to wash the dog for me."

Notice, too, how the identity of the doer of *morau* or *kureru* limits the possible uses and meanings of certain everyday expressions. You can, for example, ask another person if he/she will *kureru* for you, but since you are the one who *morau*'s, you can't ask him if he will *morau* from you, and since only you can take the initiative to *morau*, you can't ask him if you will *morau* from him. So these are possible: *Kaite kuremasu (kuremasen / kudasaimasu / kudasaimasen) ka* / "Will you please write it for me?" But you can't ask, *Kaite moraimasu (moraimasen / itadakimasu / itadakimasen) ka* / "Am I going to take the initiative to get you to write it for me?" which sounds a little like the soggy camper's lament, "Are we having fun yet?" You *can*, however, ask the other person, *Kaite moraemasu (itadakemasu) ka* / "*Can* I get you to write it for me?" = "Will it be possible for me to get you to write it for me?"

Again, since you are the one who does *morau*, you can add the subjective ending -*tai*, expressing desire, to it and make the subjective statement that you want to *morau* as in *Kaite moraitai* / "I'd like to receive from you your writing this for me" = "I'd like you to write this for me." But because the other person is the one who *kureru*'s, you can't say something like *Kaite kuretai*, which looks as though it should translate "I'd like you to write it for me" but which is in fact impossible because—even if you are a clairvoyant—you can't say "I feel that you want to give me your writing of it."

The warning about murdering your subjects by translating *-te kureru* constructions into the passive applies with even greater urgency to *-te morau* constructions. You would only see *Inu o aratte kureta* in situations where the identity of the subject of the final verb *kureta* is quite clear. But since *you* are the subject of *Inu o aratte moratta*, there can be less emphasis on the doer of the washing, so you might use the expression in contexts where the washers are not clearly specified: "I had them wash the dog for me," which slides all-too-easily into a passive such as "I had the dog washed." Beware of English "equivalents" for such forms that resort to the old "someone," too: "I had the dog washed by someone." This is not what's going on in the Japanese. The actors involved are present as zero pronouns: "I had him/her/them wash the dog for me." This may sound terrifically picky, but I guarantee that if you resort too uncritically to the passive and "someone" at this stage, a *real* someone in the text or conversation is sure to get bumped off when you have to deal with more challenging material.[2]

There'll be more on this later under the discussion of the passive.

THE CAUSATIVE, WITH AND WITHOUT DIRECTIONALS

Besides *-te itadaku* and *-te morau*, another way one person can get another to do something is with the causative. Usually, this is not a very polite way to go about getting people to do things because if you talk about causing people to perform actions, as if they are entirely subject to your will, there can be a good bit of arrogance implied. A *-te morau* construction at least implies that, although you initiated the receiving of the action, the other person did it of his own free will for your benefit.

Since we had people signing autographs in the above paragraphs, let's keep the verb "to write" as our illustration. This time, it's *kakaseru*, in which I (or another known subject, but let's keep it "I" for now) either "make" or "let" somebody else write something. In English translation, we choose either "make" or "let" depending on whether the person wants to do the writing or not. The causative form in Japanese, however, makes no such fine distinctions regarding the will of the person we are "causing" to do something, though context and meaning will usually make it clear enough. For example, if the verb is *yasumu*, made causative as *yasumaseru*, it's not likely we are going to *force* someone to rest against his will. (More on this tantalizing concept later.) Japanese people often fumble with "letting" or "making" people do things in English, precisely because the distinction is missing in the Japanese verb form.

The form may not tell us anything about whether the other person wants to be "caused" or not, but it *does* tell us that there are two people involved, one causing the other to perform the verb to which the causative ending has been added. Your textbook no doubt tells you that the person who is caused to do the action will be indicated with a *ni* or *o*, but more often than not, there won't be any overt mention of anybody since it's all clear from the context and from the verb forms themselves. Even when the causative is itself put into the *-te* form before a *kureru* or *morau*, the zero pronoun is often all that's given. As far as I'm concerned, this is where the real fun begins.

So far, we've been talking about situations in which

Mr. A makes Mr. B write something: *kakaseru*. What's going on in *kakasete kureta*? Remember that in the *kaite kureru* type of construction, the other person does both the final verb of the clause or sentence, *kureru*, and the action in the *-te* verb form for us. In *kakasete kureta*, the other person does the *kureru* for us as always but he only does the *causing* for us in the *-te* verb form: he causes *someone else* to do the writing. Here, you can have either two or three people involved. "He gave me his causing to write" does not specify who does the writing, but the context will make this clear. If we've been talking about Sally, it could mean "He gave me his causing Sally to write" ("He did me a favor and got Sally to write it," "He kindly had Sally write it for me"), but if only the two of us are involved, it could mean "He gave me his causing me to write" ("He did me a favor and let me write it," "He kindly allowed me to write it"). In any case, "He," the subject of our final verb *kureru*, does not do the writing; he only does the causing, and he does it for me.

"He" doesn't do any writing in *kakasete moratta*, either. You should recall how, in *-te morau* constructions, "I" do the receiving but the other person does the verb in the *-te* form. In *kakasete moratta*, "I" do the *morau* as always but the other person only does the causing: he still causes *someone else* to do the writing. "I got from him his causing to write" can mean either "I got from him his causing me to write" ("I got him to let me write it") or (in actual usage, the far less likely) "I got from him his causing Sally to write" ("I got him to let Sally write it," "I got him to make Sally write it.") The Japanese want to know what's going on just as much as you do, so they will not use forms like this unless the verbal or real-world context makes it clear who is involved. As long as you realize how many players the verb forms require and you look for

THE INVISIBLE MAN

them, you'll find them.

Here are a few examples of causatives with auxiliaries of giving *from* the speaker rather than *to* the speaker. Notice that they suggest situations of dominance or familiarity:

Itai me ni awasete yatta. / "I gave him the causing of him to meet up with a painful experience." = "I put him through a tough time." = "I kicked his butt."

Kakasete yatta. / "I (showed him who's boss and) made him write it."

Tomodachi ga komatte ita no de, watashi no jisho o tsukawasete ageta. / "My friend was in a pinch, so I let her use my dictionary."

Kakasete ageta. / "I let her write it."

Tarō-chan ni chotto yarasete agete kudasai. / "Please let little Tarō do it (try it, play baseball, etc.)."

Let's look at some texts, starting with an example that uses the causative by itself without any directional verbs. This is from an essay (*zuihitsu*) by Watanabe Jun'ichi, in which the writer describes his own angry outburst at a Sicilian innkeeper. Watanabe had asked the man to combine the room's two single beds into a double, but there had been no move to accommodate him. When Watanabe asked for the fifth time, he was told the "person in charge" (*kakari*) was at lunch and would do the job tomorrow— which was the day Watanabe would be checking out. At this, Watanabe blew up and yelled (among other things), *Sugu kakari o yonde kite yarasero.*[3]

Yarasero ends with a blunt imperative (*-ro*), making it a command to the listener, i.e., the innkeeper at the front desk. Here, Watanabe is ordering the innkeeper to cause somebody to *yaru*, which in this context means "to do," so together it means "make him (or her) do it." The sentence could be translated, "Go get the person in charge and make him do it." Altogether there are three people involved: the speaker issuing the command, the listener at the front desk, and the room clerk whom the listener is supposed to make put the two single beds together. Unless you take the zero pronoun into account, you might end up with translations such as these actual examples by certain unnamed acquaintances of mine:

"Call the room attendant right away." "Go call and get the person in charge quickly, goddammit!" "Call the person in charge immediately and have him come." "Immediately go and speak to the person in charge." "Hurry up and get the duty person!" "Go and tell the room clerk immediately, then come back!" "Call the front desk right now and make him do it." "Go get ahold of the attendant right now (literally, 'Call him, come back, do it!')." "Go get the person in charge and tell him to do it (*yarasero* is 'I cause you to tell him *yaro*')" (In fairness to these translators, it must be pointed out that there is an idiomatic usage giving them some difficulty. See "Go Jump in the Lake, But Be Sure to Come Back.")

Now here's a very short text with a causative in the *-te* form followed by *itadaku*, which differs from *morau* only in being more polite. The single sentence is engraved on a narrow, foot-long white plastic sign that I bought long ago in a Japanese department store to hang in my office. Its graceful black characters proclaim to anyone who can read it my shameless determination to have the day off: *Honjitsu wa yasumasete itadakimasu.* The wish it expresses is genuine enough, but that's not why I bought it. I bought it—and still love it—for its verb forms. (No kinkiness intended.)

At the time I bought it, I suppose I was feeling pleased

with myself that I could actually understand a verbal expression so different from anything in my native tongue, Serbo-Melanesian. As I've said elsewhere, one of the great pleasures in learning Japanese comes in those moments of reflection *after* you have spoken or understood one of these strange expressions automatically, and you realize that you have learned to make your mind work in ways your mother never could have imagined. Even now, after more years at this business than I care to count at the moment, such verbal agglomerations still have the power to fascinate me, and whenever they come up in class, I like to pause over them to make sure the students are getting the idea of just how outrageous Japanese can be.

Honjitsu wa yasumasete itadakimasu. Two verbs. No subjects, no objects, no agents, nobody. And the *Honjitsu wa* tells us only that these two incredible verbs are happening "today." Despite this, the sentence is both complete and perfectly clear. As the great Zen master Dōgen himself might have translated it, "Gone fishin'."

Is *that* all it means?! Well no, not literally, but it is just as much of a cliche in its culture as "Gone fishin'" or "Closed for the Day" might be in ours. It can be a lot more fun, though, if we look at it closely.

The final verb of the sentence is *itadakimasu*, which tells us that the unnamed subject is going to humbly receive something from someone more exalted. And what the subject is going to humbly receive is the exalted person's doing of the causative part of the *-te* form verb that immediately precedes the *itadakimasu*.

So, what's going on in this *yasumasete* that the more exalted person is going to do? *Yasumu* is the verb meaning "to rest," and it is in the causative form, which means that our exalted individual will cause *someone else* to rest, i.e., he is going to *let* the humble receiver do the resting.

If we go back to our final verb and call the unknown subject of that X and the exalted other person Y, we've got something like "X will humbly receive Y's letting X rest."

Now, who are X and Y? How can a sign like this, with no surrounding text, mean anything to anybody? Here, the context comes from the real world. The sign hangs in a shop window and the would-be customer finds the place closed, the sign telling him that "(We, the shopkeepers,) humbly receive (from you, the exalted customer,) (your) letting (us) rest today."

This is all phrased in tremendously polite language, but the fact remains that the shop owner is telling the customer that, whatever the customer may think of the matter, the owner is closing the shop for the day. *Itadaku* is performed by the subject, at his own discretion, and it carries the message "I take it upon myself in all humility to get from you . . ." It's like those signs "Thank you for not smoking," which always impress me as having an underlying growl that makes them even more intimidating than a plain "No Smoking."

A completely naturalized translation for the sign might simply be "Closed," though that way we lose the interesting cultural difference. Perhaps "We thank you for allowing us to have the day off" or "We appreciate your permitting us to have the day off" would begin to convey some sense of the respectful tone of the Japanese in natural-sounding English. But make no mistake about it: the owner has gone fishin'.

Now, give this one a try. It comes from a story by the writer Hoshi Shin'ichi. A door-to-door salesman has just been told by the lady of the house that, since her husband isn't home, she can't buy the automatic backscratcher he

THE INVISIBLE MAN

has been trying to sell her today. He gives up and says, *De wa, chikai uchi ni, mata o-ukagai sasete itadaku koto ni itashimashō.*[4] In the *o-ukagai sasete itadaku,* who does the *ukagai* part, the *sasete* part, the *itadaku* part?

Start from the *itadaku,* the final verb of the clause modifying *koto.* The speaker is the only one of the two present who could do *itadaku,* which the other person never does. Thus, he wants to get her to cause him to do whatever comes before the causative. *Ukagai* comes from *ukagau,* to humbly visit—again, a humble verb that only the speaker would do. A painfully literal translation of the phrase might be: "I shall humbly receive from you your allowing me to humbly visit you." A less painful version might be, "I will call upon you again if I may," which retains some of the force of the speaker's initiative implied by the *itadaku.*

Unless you keep track of the zero pronouns performing the parts of the sandwich, you might come up with such "literal" translations as these: "Please make yourself stop by for me," or "May I cause you to receive my visit again?" or "I will cause you to receive my calling on you (honorable person)," or "Perhaps you will give me letting me visit again soon," or "Please allow me to cause another visit," or "Perhaps I'll visit again, since you've caused me to (by not buying the product)."

There are some real problems here. If you recognize them, take a hard look at your textbook.

PASSIVES, PASSIVICATION, AND THE PASSIVE-CAUSATIVE

The biggest problem surrounding the Japanese passive comes not so much from the form itself as from the overuse of the English passive to interpret active Japanese statements, a bad habit that can be developed long before the textbook ever gets to the passive.

I spend so much energy warning my students not to translate active Japanese verbs into English passives that one bright young fellow named John Briggs invented a grammatical term for my own exclusive use: "passivication." (He was so pleased with himself for coining the word that he grew a moustache.) Now, what is wrong with passivication? The answer is almost shockingly simple. If you make an active verb passive, you tend to forget that the active verb had a subject. In fact, getting rid of that subject is precisely what we often use the passive for in English. In a fit of modesty, an author may tell us in his preface, "This book was written during the Klench Rebellion," making "book" the subject, rather than coming right out and admitting that "I wrote this book" himself. This is the same process that killed off our subject when our dog was washed for us above in the discussions of *kureru* and *morau*.

An English verb is in the active voice when its subject is the actor, while a verb is in the passive voice when the subject receives the action. "Melvin ate his french fries" is active, while "Melvin was eaten by his french fries" is passive (if not tragic).

Note here that it is the relationship of the subject and the verb that determines the difference. Let's look at a few more. "Laura was arrested." Laura is the subject, and the verb is being done to her, so it's passive. If we further specify that "Laura was arrested by the police," Laura is still the subject, and the police are the agents, the ones by whom Laura has the verb done to her. "The police arrested Laura." Now it is the police that are doing the verb, so they are the subject and Laura is the object. If the subject is doing the verb, it is an active verb. We should also note that if the subject is doing the verb *to* something, the verb is not only active but transitive: the police didn't simply "arrest," they arrested *Laura*. If, when they came for her, "Laura ran," she would have been doing an intransitive verb: she wouldn't have been running *something*, just running.

In English, only a transitive verb can become passive. Japanese is a little different, but we don't have to go into that yet. The important thing to remember is that, both in English and Japanese, transitive verbs always have subjects and objects: "Cameron slugged the intruder," "Baskin married Robbins," "Bob got it," "It got Bob," "Iwata killed Terry," "She counted them," "They met her." The one big difference, of course, is that in Japanese those pronominal subjects and objects won't be mentioned in the sentence.

Almost invariably, when a student has trouble finding the subject of an active verb, he or she will panic and quickly transform the verb into an English passive to make the problem go away. And when the all-important connection between subject and verb is lost, the sentence enters the twilight zone.

Just to confuse things further, Japanese has a different kind of passive, using the same passive ending, *rareru*, often somewhat misleadingly called the "suffering (or adversative) passive," in which the subject does not have the verb done to it but "suffers" the doing of the verb. Although the form is often used in unpleasant situations, genuine "suffering" is not inherent to it, and in fact the distress usually has to be explicitly expressed with an additional *komatta* or *hidoi me ni atta* or some such complaint. The important thing is that the subject gets passively *rareru*'ed, but it doesn't get acted upon by the rest of the verb. This is tough because there's nothing quite like it in English, but we just make it that much tougher on ourselves when we lose track of the unnamed subject. Let's see how this works by stealing a suitcase.

1. *Kaban o nusunda.* / "X stole the suitcase."
2. *Kaban ga nusumareta.* / "The suitcase was stolen."
3. *Kaban o nusumareta.* / "X suffered the Y-stole-the suitcase."

Number 1 contains an ordinary active transitive verb and it makes complete sense only in a context that tells us who X is. As a transitive verb, *nusumu* must have both a subject and an object. Here, the sentence doesn't name the subject because it assumes we already know who the subject is. This is a typical unstressed statement using the silent Japanese zero pronoun. This could be "I, you, he, she, we, you-plural, or they stole the suitcase," depending on the identity of the perpetrator (i.e., the subject).

Number 2 is like the English passive (and, in fact, the widespread knowledge of English in Japan has probably contributed to the acceptability of the form). The subject is named, marked with the subject marker *ga*, and the whole verb is done to it: "The suitcase was stolen."

Number 3 is an example of the Japanese "suffering passive," a form that can be used with both transitive and intransitive verbs, and thus one that is very different from the English passive. The subject is the one who gets *rareru*'ed whether the passive Japanese verb is transitive or intransitive. For example: *Ame ni furarete komatta* / "Being fallen on by rain, I was distressed" = "Damn, I got rained on." The passive is working the same way in sentence number 3. Marked by *o*, however, the suitcase is labeled as an object, and this means it cannot be *rareru*'ed (or, here, for phonetic reasons, *mareru*'ed): only a subject can be *rareru*'ed, and *kaban* cannot be a subject when followed by *o*. For this reason, the sentence cannot mean "The suitcase was stolen."

So, what was stolen?

Well, as a matter of fact, the suitcase *was* stolen.

So why don't we just translate it "The suitcase was stolen" and be done with it?

Well, if *your* suitcase had been stolen and the police didn't try to find it for *you*, you'd not only be very resentful, you'd probably never get your suitcase back. The suitcase itself may have been stolen, but the victim of the crime was *you*, and the use of the Japanese passive tells you that, whether it is mentioned or not, there is a subject who is "suffering" the doing of the verb. Used with a transitive verb, the passive is a neat way of saying that the victim/subject "suffered" the doing of the verb *by* someone else (the agent, marked with a *ni* when mentioned, though often a zero pronoun) *to* something else (the object, marked with an *o* when present, also often a zero pronoun). The subject remains *you* (or whoever else the context has established as the subject), so *you* get *rareru*'ed by somebody, but you don't get stolen.[5]

"Pardon me, officer, but I've just been *rareru*'ed," you say to the policeman.

"Oh, sorry to hear that, sir, but what were you *rareru*'ed?"

"I was *rareru*'ed somebody's having stolen my suitcase."

"How's that again?"

"I was stolen my suitcase!"

"What an odd way to put it!"

"Of course it's odd. I'm Japanese, and that's how we phrase these things when our English is a little shaky!"

As the officer says, your expression may be odd, but it's perfectly clear. From it, he knows that you are the victim, that someone did the stealing, and that the someone stole your suitcase. *Kaban o nusumareta*, then, is a clear statement involving you, the robber, and the suitcase, though only the suitcase is actually mentioned.

In translating a sentence like *Kaban o nusumareta*, don't resort to something like "The suitcase was stolen and I was distressed." The suitcase was *not* passively stolen: the unmentioned "I" was the one passively affected. Much closer to the original would be a "literal" equivalent such as, "I was unfavorably affected by someone's having stolen the suitcase," or "I suffered someone's stealing my suitcase." These are pretty awkward, of course, and not for consumption beyond the walls of the classroom. Since "I was stolen my suitcase" is probably even worse, you might finally want to go as far as "Oh, no, they stole my suitcase!" or "Damn! The rats took my suitcase!" or any number of other expressions of dismay befitting the overall tone of the translation.

Here, by the way, is an example in which the "suffering passive" implies no suffering. The narrator of Murakami Haruki's "Tony Takitani" informs us that Tony's father was a somewhat widely known jazz trombonist in the prewar days: *Kare no chichioya wa Takitani Shōzaburō to iu, senzen kara sukoshi wa **na o shirareta** jazu-toronbōn-fuki datta* / "His father was a jazz trombonist by the name of Takitani Shōzaburō who 'suffered' the knowing of his name somewhat from before the war."[6]

Much of the trouble with the passive, as I have said, starts long before it ever makes its appearance in the textbook. Let me add a word here to Japanese language teachers on this matter while the rest of you leave the room.

If students have been arbitrarily translating active Japanese into either active or passive English depending upon whether the subject is more obvious or less obvious, they will not see that the introduction of the Japanese passive voice allows them to say things in a whole new way. One good method to prepare students for the coming of the Japanese passive is to demand that all translating in the course before the passive is introduced, even at the most elementary level, be done into the English active voice, passive translation being called to their attention as an error or, when unavoidable, as a poor compromise. (This will also provide grammar-starved students with some grounding in what the passive is before they have to deal with it in Japanese.)

This might put some strain on the naturalness of the translating, but it would help students to remember that active verbs always have doers. Even something as naturally passivized as the verb *iu* should be kept active.

All right, students can come back in now. *Japanese: The Spoken Language* says "The verbal *iu* has two basic meanings: 'say' and 'be named' or 'be called,'" but one illustration further down the page gives a good approach for avoiding such misleading passivication: *Kore wa, Nihongo de nan to iu n desu ka* / "What is it you call this in Japanese?"[7]

Who, we might ask, is the "you" in this translation? Certainly it isn't the person being addressed by the speaker. It's people in general, the same ones who show up in "They say that falling in love is wonderful," where they are called "they." By now, of course, we know that "they" in Japanese is the zero pronoun, and that is exactly who is doing the verb *iu*. They do it again in the phrase *Itō to iu hito*, which most of us (or at least those of us who had seen the movie "A Fish Called Wanda") would translate "a man called Itō," but which, in the original, is closer to "a man they call Itō." Better to get away from the Japanese entirely with something like "a man by the name of Itō" than to passivize.

THE INVISIBLE MAN

Probably the most widely known passivized translation from Japanese is one that has been made from the inscription engraved on the monument in Hiroshima to those who were killed by the atomic bomb.[8] The original inscription, which contains what may be the most broadly inclusive zero pronoun, is a sobering one, with far greater impact in the Japanese original than in its weakened English translation:

> *Yasuraka ni nemutte kudasai. Ayamachi wa kurikae-shimasen kara.* / "Rest in peace, for X will not repeat the mistake."[9]

This has been rendered, "Rest it peace, for the mistake will not be repeated," which is far less problematical than the original. "*Who* will not repeat the mistake?" people wanted to know when the monument was unveiled. "And who made the mistake in the first place—the Americans when they dropped the bomb, or the Japanese when they started the war?" The transitive Japanese verb in the active voice calls for a subject—a responsible actor. The passivized translation makes far less stringent demands. With its unnamed subject, the Japanese sentence seems discreetly to avoid placing the blame on anyone, but it is far more thought-provoking than the English translation would suggest, for the inescapable conclusion to the unavoidable search for a subject is "we."

Many intransitive Japanese verbs present another type of problem, more one of translation than understanding. These verbs often demand the English passive for natural translation. Someone can "straighten up" a room with *katazukeru*, but in Japanese we can also speak of the room as "becoming straight," *katazuku*, without reference to who does the straightening, even as a zero pronoun. Then it is difficult to avoid saying something like, "The room has been put in order." *Naoru* is another tricky verb, easy to translate when used with people—*Naotta* / "He got well," but hard to avoid passivizing when describing broken radios, which in English we do not characterize as having "gotten well": *Naotta* / "It got fixed" = "It was repaired."

Another form that is virtually impossible not to passivize in translation is a transitive verb inflected with *-te aru*. *Mado **ga** shimete aru* (or *Mado **o** shimete aru*, putting more emphasis on a person's having done the deed) may literally mean "The window is in a state of someone's having shut it," but the passive is unavoidable if we are going to keep the window as the subject in a normal English translation: "The window has been shut." Otherwise, to make the translation natural, we would have to turn the window into an object, "Someone has shut the window." The trouble here is that this particular Japanese construction focuses on the state of things *after* someone has performed an active verb, something we just don't do in English. It is neither passive ("The window was shut") nor active ("Someone shut the window"), but it forces us to choose one or the other in English. Again, in *preparation* for the eventual appearance of the true passive, students should be informed when this construction appears that it is not passive and that they are being allowed to passivize it in translation only as an expedient.

And finally, some good news. If you've got the causative and the passive down, the passive-causative is easy. The form is mainly used in complaints by the speaker that he was forced by someone to do something, so the subject is almost always "I." "I" is the one who gets *rareru'*ed, and of course someone else does the causing.

Being fired from a job, for example, is commonly described by the firee in terms of his having been forced to quit, *yameru* ("to quit") becoming *yame-sase-rareta* ("I suffered X's forcing me to quit"). If the president of the company is to be named as the one who did it, we get *Shachō* **ni** *yamesaserareta*, but his participation is implied even without such specific reference. In the case of a transitive verb like *toru* ("to take"), made into the sentence *Toraserareta* ("I suffered X's forcing me to take it" = "I was made to take it"), not only "I" and the one who forced "I" but also the thing "I" took can be present only as zero pronouns. Keeping score of the players works the same way in third-person narratives.

THE NATURAL POTENTIAL

I said in the introduction to this book that, "All too often, students are subtly encouraged to think that Japanese verbs just 'happen,' without subjects, deep within some Oriental fog. In the world represented by Japanese, actions 'occur,' but nobody does them," and I've said a lot since then to lay to rest such "twilight zone" notions about the Japanese language. Now I take it all back. There really *is* a twilight zone in Japanese, and the "natural potential" is it, that misty crossroads where the passive and potential intersect, where things happen spontaneously or naturally. Another term for the "natural potential" (*shizen kanō*) is the "spontaneous passive" (*jihatsu ukemi*).

We encounter this form most commonly when an essayist, after supposedly regaling us with objective facts, suddenly ends a sentence with *kangaerareru* or *omowareru* or *omoeru*, any of which would seem to mean "it is thinkable" or "it is thought," but not "I think." What is he doing? Ducking responsibility for his own ideas?

"Passive and potential forms are sometimes used in a way which might strike the English speaker as strange," says Anthony Alfonso. "When something is *left*, or *thought*, or even *done* involuntarily or naturally by a person, the action is described in an OBJECTIVE manner and by means of either the potential form or the passive form with a potential meaning."[10]

Take, for example, this somewhat spooky recollection of a childhood incident by the narrator of a story called "Man-Eating Cats." The day his cat disappeared into the garden's pine tree, he says, he sat on the verandah until late in the evening, unable to take his eyes off the upper branches of the tree in the brilliant moonlight. *Tokidoki sono eda no naka de, tsuki no hikari o obite neko no me ga kirari to hikatta yō ni omoeta. Demo sore wa boku no sakkaku ka mo shirenakatta.* "Every now and then, the cat's eyes *seemed to be* flashing in the light of the moon. Maybe it was just a hallucination of mine."[11] The italicized phrase translates the natural potential expression *yō ni omoeta*, which certainly does not mean "I was able to think that . . . " and certainly does mean something more like "It seemed that . . . ," "One couldn't help feeling that," "One could not but think that . . . ," etc.

I'm not sure if such a description is entirely "objective," but it does seem to be removed from the observer's exclusively subjective domain, perhaps floating somewhere in the middle between pure subjectivity and pure objectivity. The implication is that the environment naturally leads the speaker to think or feel something. These forms don't translate properly as either passive ("It was thought by me") or potential ("I could think that").

A few more examples: When a sad occasion brings forth an involuntary gush of tears, the verb *naku*, "to cry," is routinely inflected as a potential, *nakeru*, as in *Nakete kichatta* / "I just couldn't help crying." When a Japanese fisherman pulls a fish out of the water he doesn't take the credit for it as English speakers do. Instead of shouting

"I've got one!" he inflects the verb *tsuru* (to fish) with the potential ending and says *Tsureta!* / "It has spontaneously caught itself on my line!" And when a Japanese writer talks about the successful completion of a novel, he will often say *Shōsetsu ga kaketa*, meaning not boastfully "I was able to write it," but far more modestly, "It was writable," "It wrote itself."

Good luck with this one.

*

Here is a chart summarizing the forms treated in this chapter. These are all *complete sentences*, with implied subjects, objects, and agents, using the transitive verb *kaku* (to write), which appeared prominently in the explanations above, and supplying a *tegami* in two cases to illustrate the different uses of the passive. I have put all the verb forms into the perfective *-ta* form as you would most likely encounter them, in statements about actual actions having been performed by known people, and translated the examples using first-person singular subjects and masculine third-person singular pronouns for simplicity, employing the feminine at two points to indicate the presence of a third party. The emphasis here is on the number of players involved and direction of the action, not levels of respect.

Kaita.	I wrote it.
Kaite yatta/ageta.	I wrote it for him.
Kaite kureta/kudasatta.	He wrote it for me.
Kaite moratta/itadaita.	I got him to write it for me.
Kakaseta.	I made/let him write it.
Kakasete kureta/kudasatta.	He did me the favor of making/letting her/me write it.
Kakasete moratta/itadaita.	I got him to let me write it, or

	I got him to make/let her write it.
Kakasete ageta/yatta.	I let/made him write it.
Kakareta.	It was written, or I was adversely affected by his having written it.
Tegami ga kakareta.	The letter was written.
Tegami o kakareta.	I suffered the consequences of his writing the letter.
Kakaserareta.	I was forced by him to write it.
Kaite atta.	It had been written. (false passive)
Kaketa.	It successfully wrote itself.

The Explainers
Kara Da, Wake Da, No Da

Notwithstanding their reputation as lovers of silence, the Japanese do an awful lot of explaining. Sometimes it seems as if they try to explain *everything*. They certainly do a lot more explaining than we do in English, even to the point of explaining when there's almost nothing to explain, just to give the impression that they're explaining objective reality when in fact they're just stating their personal opinions like everybody else. Now, after having given you an opening paragraph like this, I've got an awful lot of explaining to do myself.

What I'm talking about are those little phrases that seem to pop up at the ends of sentences or clauses to tell you that what you are reading is an explanation of what the author said in the sentence before, or that what you are hearing is an explanation of the real-world situation for those who are standing in it: *kara da*, *wake da*, and *no da*. (Of course, there are differences in nuance among these forms, but they all "explain" what came before. Note, too, that all *da*'s can be interchanged with *desu* or *de aru*—or even dropped—depending on style.) Let's start with an old standby: *Kore wa pen desu* / "And this: it's a pen." We have to get this basic building block straight before we start wrapping whole little sentences like this around bigger ones. Be sure to read "*Wa* and *Ga*" if you don't know why the translation isn't simply "This is a pen."

In *Kore wa pen desu*, the subject of *desu* is not *kore* but the zero pronoun that Japanese uses instead of "it." If we just want to say "It's a pen," we drop *Kore wa* and get the complete sentence, *Pen desu*. "It's a dog" = *Inu desu*, "It's a desk" = *Tsukue desu*. In other words, in the basic *A wa B desu* / A = B construction, the *A wa* part is often going to disappear, so when you see a sentence in the form of "Noun *desu*" (or "Noun *da*" or "Noun *de aru*"), that noun is the B part of an *A wa B desu* construction.

When you find a sentence ending with a final verb or adjective + *kara da* ("It's because") construction, the *kara* is acting just like the B noun in an "(A *wa*) B *da*" sentence.[1] Instead of *Nemui kara hayaku néru* / "Since I'm sleepy I'm going to bed early," you could have: *Hayaku neru. Nemui kara (da).* / "I'm going to bed early. That's because I'm sleepy," or *Hayaku neru. Naze nara, nemui kara da.* / "I'm going to bed early. Why? Because I'm sleepy" or any number of variations in which the explanation follows the main statement. The subject of the *da* here is the zero pronoun "that" or "it"; i.e., the fact that I'm going to bed early. Here is a straightforward example from a story by Murakami Haruki about the mysterious disappearance of an elephant:

Sono shōgakusei-tachi ga zō no saigo no mokugeki-sha de, sono go zō no sugata o me ni shita mono wa inai—to shinbun kiji wa katatte ita. **Naze nara** *rokuji no sairen ga naru to, shiiku-gakari wa zō no hiroba no mon o shimete, hitobito ga naka ni hairenai yō ni shite shimau* **kara da**.

These pupils were the last eyewitnesses, and no one had seen the elephant after that, according to the article. **This was because** the keeper always closed the gate to the elephant enclosure when the six o'clock siren blew, making it impossible for people to enter.[2]

Notice how *naze nara* and *kara da* work together as a pair ("Why is this? It's because . . ."). I've conflated this common construction in the phrase "this was because." For more on this pair and pairs in general, see the chapter "Warning: This Language Works Backwards." Notice, too, that these explanatory expressions, being comments upon something said earlier, powerfully imply the presence of a human mind doing the commenting. The construction shows up in situations in which someone is evaluating or judging or preaching, and in positive statements there is a strong presumption that the speaker or writer has a better grasp of objective reality than the listener: "Look, it's this, it's this, it's this, this is what you should do, I'm telling you the truth."

Here are a couple of examples of *kara da* from essays by the novelist Mishima Yukio, who was always convinced of his rightness and who used the form so frequently that he finally lost his head. The first concerns his feelings at the time he wrote his first "novel" (the irony is his),

Kamen no kokuhaku (Confessions of a Mask):

> . . . *sukoshi nen-iri ni jibun no shinpen o aratte mitai ki ga suru.* **Naze nara** *kono shōsetsu to, sore kara sūnen-go no saisho no sekai-ryokō to de, watashi no henreki jidai wa hobo owatta to kangaerareru* **kara de aru***.*

I would like to examine my private life here in some detail. **That is because** my years of wandering would seem to have come pretty much to an end with this "novel" and with the world tour I made a few years later.[3]

This next one doesn't use *naze nara* but sets up a *wa*-topic to be explained:

> *"Hanazakari no mori" shohan-bon no jobun nado o ima yonde mite iya na no wa,* . . . *nan-wari ka no jibun ni, chiisa na chiisa na opochunisuto no kage o hakken suru* **kara de aru***.*

That I feel sick now when I read such things as the preface to the first edition of [my] "Hanazakari no mori" . . . *is because* I discover in a certain part of myself the image of a petty opportunist.[4]

One sentence in the old Hibbett and Itasaka textbook that always threw students for a loop was this one at the beginning of a paragraph written by Funahashi Seiichi:

> *Iin no daibubun ga, Nihon-jin no seikatsu kara kanji o nakushite shimaō to iu kangae no hito bakari de atta* **kara da***.*

The majority of the committee members were made up

only of those who wanted to eliminate *kanji* from the life of the Japanese once and for all **kara da**.[5]

The problem was always what to do with that *kara da* hanging on the end. Well, if we see that *kara da* means "It's because," we have to start looking for the zero pronoun subject of the *da*. The antecedent of the "it," then, has to have been established somewhere before this sentence, but since this is the first sentence in the paragraph, that forces us into the previous paragraph. With a horrible wrenching in the gut, we come to realize that Funahashi Seiichi has purposely thrown a paragraph break in just where it can best disrupt the logical connection of his ideas. In the last sentence of the previous paragraph, he tells us that he was always viewed as something of a heretic on the committee, and he continues in the new paragraph, "That's because the majority of the committee members . . . etc."

This teaches us a couple of things. First, never trust Japanese paragraphing (or punctuation) to work as it does in English. Second, never ignore those *kara da*'s at the ends of sentences because these are the very things that are going to connect a sentence to what came before it. In fact, the *kara da* IS the sentence, and everything leading up to it is just a modifier. The main clause of *Iin no daibubun ga, Nihon-jin no seikatsu kara kanji o nakushite shimaō to iu kangae no hito bakari de atta* **kara da** is nothing more nor less than *kara da*, which becomes, in English, "That is because," the main verb of the sentence being *da* and the subject of *da* being the zero pronoun pointing back to the previous sentence. Don't let this throw you, it's really very simple. When a long sentence ends with a "That's because," it means "That [i.e., what was just said in the previous sentence] is because of everything in this sentence that precedes the *kara da*."

All of these little explainers at the ends of sentences work this way. They are the main sentence, and everything else modifies them.

In one sense, *wake da* and *no da* are even easier to understand than *kara da* because *wake* and *no* are clearly nouns (as *kara* is not), and they are being modified by what precedes them just as surely as *fūsen* is modifed by *akai* in the phrase *akai fūsen* / red balloon. *Akai fūsen da* / "It is a red balloon."

Unlike *no*, which is an element of grammatical structure (probably evolved from the noun *mono*, "thing"), *wake* is an independent noun, defined by Kenkyusha with such terms as "meaning, sense; reason, cause, grounds." *Sore wa dō iu **wake** desu ka* / "What do you mean by that?" and ***wake** o hanasu* / "to tell the reason" = "to explain" are examples of this usage. Coming at the ends of sentences, both *wake da* and *no da* mean "the reason for that is" or, more simply, "it means" or "that means," or "it's that" or "it's not that" (in the sense of "It's not that I'm a big fan of Van Damme or anything; it's just that I like the music in his films") with the "it" or "that" being a zero pronoun pointing to what has been said in the sentence before or something in the objective situation observable by both speaker and listener. Kenkyusha gives us some good examples of the negative usage:

*Warui imi de itta **no de** wa nai* / "It's not that I said it with a bad meaning" = "I meant no ill will."
*Betsu-ni fukai imi ga atte sō itta **wake de** wa nai* / "It's not that I said so with a deep meaning" = "I didn't mean anything serious when I said so."

These, interestingly enough, are to be found under the

definition of *imi*, which means "meaning." Notice that these two sentences are basically saying the same thing, and that the *no* and *wake* are perfectly interchangable. (It would be unnatural but understandable to replace either of them with the word *imi* itself, since both are commenting on the "meaning" or "significance" of what was, by implication, said before: "The meaning of what I just said is not that so-and-so but such-and-such.)

In speech, *no da* (contracted to *n da* or *n desu* or simply *no* in feminine speech) endings often refer not to anything that has been said but to the objective situation, there for both speaker and listener to observe. Anthony Alfonso illustrates this vividly with the following contrasting pair, both members of which could be translated "Is it interesting?" *Omoshiroi desu ka* is a question you would ask a person about a book he owns. *Omoshiroi n desu ka* is a question you would "ask of someone [reading a book] whose attention is visibly absorbed, or who has broken into a smile or a laugh."[6]

N desu ka is a question—a complete, self-contained sentence implying "Does our shared experience mean . . . ?" In texts, the "shared experience" is the context that has been established to that point, usually in the preceding sentence. Everything preceding the *n* or *no* is a dependent clause modifying the noun *no*. It is a mistake to call *no da* an "extended predicate," as if it were an extension to the predicate, just a little more information about the subject with which the sentence started. By the time you get into the *no da*, the subject has changed. For example:

> *Sono toki mo, watashi wa tabun kokoro no naka de sono ki to hanashi o shite ita no darō to omou.* / "I think I must have been conversing with the tree in my heart that time, too."[7]

Much more literally: "That time, too, as for me, (I) probably in my heart was doing a conversation with that tree (it) probably is, (I) think." Whether or not you agree with me about zero pronouns, "I" is clearly the subject of *shite ita* ("I was doing a conversation") but that is where the predicate about "I" ends, and we enter a whole new *sentence*, "It is," following which the *wa*-topic re-emerges to comment, "(I) think."

The main verb of a sentence ending *no da* is *da*, and the subject of the *da* is not the subject of the clause that modifies *no*. The subject of *da* is the zero pronoun referring to the established context, whether the context is a statement or a real-world situation shared by speaker and listener, or an earlier statement shared by writer and reader.

This is true even of so brief an utterance as *Omoshiroi n desu ka* / "Is it [your laughing, snorting, drooling] that it [the book] is interesting?" *Omoshiroi*, which modifies *n*, has its own subject, the zero pronoun standing for the book, while the subject of *desu* is all those unseemly actions noted in the brackets, equally unverbalized. (Lest there be some confusion, note that the *desu* in *Omoshiroi desu ka* is simply a polite lengthener after the adjective, while the one after the *n* is the copula, "Does A = B?" When we take away politeness, *Omoshiroi?* and *Omoshiroi ka* are as blunt as we can make the question *Omoshiroi desu ka. Omoshiroi no ka* and *Omoshiroi no?* are blunt or familiar versions of *Omoshiroi n desu ka*. Here, the copula is routinely dropped, but it shows up again in macho positive statements: *Omoshiroi n da*.)

I recently came across the following forbidding, *no da*-studded passage in a list of rules for Japanese high school students studying in America:

*Moshi, mina-san ga Amerika de wa ōi-ni asobimakutte yarō to iu kangae dake de kita **no deshitara**, Amerika ni ite wa narimasen. Amerika e wa Eigo no benkyō, Amerika-jin no kurashiburi, Amerika to iu kuni no bunka o manabu tame ni kita **no de atte**, asobi ni kita **no de wa arimasen kara**.*

If it [the meaning of your being here] is that you have come to America only to have a good time, then you should not be here. Because it's that you are here to study English and learn about American culture, it's not that you are here to play.

Interestingly, this was translated into Japanese from an English original that had no such overtly explanatory or didactic elements but which were felt to be necessary by the Japanese translator. The English original read simply: "If you have come here only to have a good time, then you should not be here. You are here to study English and learn about American culture, not to play." In the Japanese text, the authoritarian writer is there, judging, explaining, and wagging her (yes, "her"!) finger at the hapless high school kids who probably do want to study English but ought to be able to have a little fun, too.

One highly explanatory paragraph from Murakami Haruki's story about the disappearing elephant provides us with some fine examples of these usages (and a couple of *tame*'s for good measure; see "Taming *Tame*" for more). The passage is a little long, but it demonstrates the structures in a developing context:

Zō ga machi (tsumari boku no sunde iru machi da) ni hikitorareru koto ni natta no mo, sono rōrei no tame datta. Machi no kōgai ni atta chiisa na dōbutsu-en ga

keiei-nan o riyū ni heisa sareta toki, dōbutsu-tachi wa
dōbutsu-torihiki chūkai-gyōsha no te o tōshite zenkoku
*no dōbutsu-en ni hikitorarete itta **no da** ga, sono zō*
dake wa toshi o torisugite iru tame ni, hikiuke-te o
mitsukeru koto ga dekinakatta. Dono dōbutsu-en mo
sude ni jūbun na dake no kazu no zō o shoyū shite ita
shi, ima ni mo shinzō-hossa o okoshite shinde shi-
maisō na yoboyobo no zō o hikitoru yō na monozuki
de yoyū no aru dōbutsu-en nante hitotsu mo nakatta
***no da**. Sonna **wake** de, sono zō wa nakama no*
dōbutsu-tachi ga minna ippiki-nokorazu sugata o
kesshite shimatta haikyo no gotoki dōbutsu-en ni, nani
o suru to mo naku—to itte mo motomoto toku ni
*nanika o shite ita to iu **wake** de wa nai **no da***
keredo—sankagetsu ka yonkagetsu no aida tatta hitori
de inokoritsuzukete ita.

The elephant's advanced age is what led to its being
adopted by the town (the town I live in). *That is to say
that,* when the little zoo in the suburbs suffered the
closing of its doors due to financial problems, the animals were taken in by zoos throughout the country
through the mediation of an animal dealer, but because
that one elephant was too old, it was impossible to find
anyone to take it in. *That is to say that* the zoos all
had plenty of elephants, and there was not one single
zoo that had the wherewithal to take in, on a whim, a
feeble, old elephant that looked as if it might die of a
heart attack at any moment. *For that reason,* the elephant stayed alone for nearly four months in the decaying zoo from which all of its companions had
without exception disappeared, with nothing to do—
though saying this, *it is not that I mean that* it especially had anything to do before.[8]

This is a grammatical translation that not only forgoes any sense of style in the English but also raises the question of what all those explanations are doing there—some of them sounding rather forced. To be sure, a stylistically smoother English version is probably not going to leave much sign of the explanatory phraseology. For example:

The elephant's age is what led to its being adopted by our town. When financial problems caused the little zoo in the suburbs to close its doors, an animal dealer found places for the animals with zoos throughout the country, but no one wanted to take such an old elephant. The zoos all had plenty of elephants, apparently, and not one of them was willing to take in a feeble old thing that looked as if it might die of a heart attack at any moment. And so, after all of its companions had disappeared, the elephant stayed alone in the decaying zoo for nearly four months with nothing to do—not that it had anything to do before.

Granted, I may have smoothed over more than I had a right to, but what has happened to those overt verbalizations of explanation? Well, often, we just don't say such things in normal English. Who needs 'em? Remember that I said before that both *Omoshiroi desu ka* and *Omoshiroi n desu ka* could be translated, "Is it interesting?" Typically, in English, we don't distinguish verbally between the two situations, at least not by such a subtle shift in phraseology. *Omoshiroi n desu ka* might come out "Interesting, huh?" or "Hey, I see you like it" or "Jeez, Frank, you're making a mess of that shirt," but Japanese is routinely going to both ask for and offer explanations of contexts far more often than English does.

No da or *no de aru* shows up frequently in texts, especially expository texts in which the writer is trying to convince you he has a handle on the truth. Some writers will bombard you with them, telling you at the end of virtually every sentence, "The objectively true explanation of what I just said is . . ." *No da* is not functioning in such cases as some kind of amorphous emphatic additive but always with its explanatory function, whether there is really anything to explain or not. I.e., it is functioning as a rhetorical device. Thus, when a writer of fiction gives us a narrator who speaks as an essayist or anthologizer or clipper of newspaper columns, such as the narrator of Murakami's story of the vanishing elephant, we get a lot more *no da*'s than in a descriptive piece by the same author—or a descriptive passage in the same piece—in which, say, a little, green monster burrows its way to the surface of the heroine's garden. The *no da*'s are constant reminders of the presence of the narrator: observing, questioning, judging, and often subtly hinting to us that he or she knows more than we do. So watch it.

PART
TWO

Out in Left Field

The Johnny Carson *Hodo*

As we go to press, the day is fast approaching when Johnny carson will finally retire from late-night television. This will be a sad moment for the teaching of Japanese— or at least for the teaching of the use of the quantitative nouns *hodo* and *kurai* in positive expressions. Students seem to catch on to the use of these words in negative sentences ("There is no straight man as overweight as Ed McMahon," etc.), but when Carson goes, that may end our only hope for a clear conceptualization of the positive uses of *hodo*.

All About Particles (Power Japanese, p. 66) provides examples of both kinds of usage. For the easy negative type:

> *Kotoshi wa kyonen **hodo** samuku nai desu.* / "This year is not as cold as last year."

For the harder positive type we find:

> *Kyō wa benkyō ga dekinai **hodo** tsukareta.* / "Today I'm so tired that I can't study."

Extensive research has demonstrated that the soundest illumination of this second usage is offered at irregular intervals by Johnny Carson, normally early in the show, during the monologue. At some point, Carson will make a statement involving an extreme condition, such as how hot or cold the weather is or how bad the economy is, to which the well-trained audience responds, for example, "How cold *is* it?" or "How bad *is* it?" Carson's answer illustrates the *extent* to which his original statement is true. When the audience asks about the economy, "How bad *is* it?" he might respond with such an allegedly clever rejoinder as, "It's *so* bad that Organized Crime had to lay off ten judges," or "It's *so* bad that oysters are producing fake pearls."[1]

"So . . . that . . ." is the key to interpreting positive statements of extent using *hodo* (or the virtually equivalent *gurai* or *kurai*).[2] Try to break the habit of mechanically using the word "extent."

If we apply the Carson method to clarifying the sentence in which the student tells us how tired he is, we can ask, like the audience, "How tired *are* you?" To which he answers like Johnny, "I'm *so* tired that studying is impossible"—not a particularly amusing rejoinder, but scarcely inferior to the fake pearls.

The important point is to note first what the central statement is without the *hodo* construction. If we throw out the *hodo* and the clause that modifies it, we end up with a simple positive statement, *Tsukareta* / "I'm tired." (The subject of *tsukareta* is, of course, "I" [the zero pronoun in Japanese], not *kyō* / "today," which is a time topic.) The *hodo* signals us to ask the speaker, "How tired *are* you?" To which he has already replied, "I'm *so* tired that I have this modifying clause hanging on me"—no—"I'm *so* tired that I can't study."

Thus, when you encounter a *hodo* expression followed by a positive statement and you have trouble figuring out the exact relationship of the parts before and after the *hodo*, put yourself into the place of Johnny Carson's audience and ask, "How much did you do your final statement?" Then quickly switch to Johnny and answer, "I did it *so* much that what-I-said-before."

Here are some examples, several with negative endings before the *hodo* but all with positive final statements:[3]

1. [*Yasumu hima ga nai hodo*] *hatarakimasu.* He works. How much does he work? He works *so* much that he has no time to rest.
2. *Kono shigoto wa* [*kodomo de mo dekiru hodo*] *yasashii desu.* This job is easy. How easy is it? It's *so* easy that even a child can do it.
3. [*Yoru nemuru koto ga dekinai hodo*] *shinpai shimashita.* I worried. How much did I worry? I worried *so* much I couldn't sleep at night.
4. [*Ōbā mo iranai hodo*] *atatakai desu.* It's warm. How warm is it? It's *so* warm you don't need an overcoat.
5. [*Nakitai hodo*] *komatta.* I was upset. How upset was I? I was *so* upset I wanted to cry.
6. *Ano hito wa* [*tsukaikirenai hodo*] *kane ga aru.* He has money. How much money does he have? He has *so* much money that he can't possibly spend it all.

Now, just in case I assumed too much regarding *hodo* with negative statements, let's apply a similar approach to a few examples:

Mizu wa [*biru hodo*] *oishiku nai.*

Take the *hodo* clause out, and you have the main clause:

Water is not good-tasting.

In other words, we're talking about "water" first and foremost, and are comparing it with the thing in the *hodo* clause.

Once you've isolated the main clause, the *hodo* signals you to ask the un-Carsonesque question: *As* good-tasting *as* what?

To which the answer is: Water is not *as* good-tasting *as* beer.

A couple more examples, including one to go with the beer:

> *Migi no me wa [hidari hodo] akaku nai.* The right eye is not red. Not *as* red *as* what? The right eye is not *as* red *as* the left.
>
> *Konshū no shiken wa [senshū no hodo] muzukashiku nai.* This week's exam will not be difficult. Not *as* difficult *as* what? This week's exam will not be *as* difficult *as* last week's.

[*Sore hodo*] *omoshiroku nai desu yo.* It (zero pronoun) is not interesting. Not *as* interesting *as* what? It is not *as* interesting *as* that. This can work like the English idiom, with no clear antecedent to either *sore* or "that": "It's not all that interesting." "Say, how was that flick, 'Double Impact'?" "Oh, it wasn't that interesting."

Kanji

Kanji are tough. Kanji are challenging. Kanji are mysterious and fun and maddening. Kanji comprise one of the greatest stumbling blocks faced by Westerners who want to become literate in Japanese. But kanji have nothing to do with grammar or sentence structure or thought patterns or the Japanese world view, and they are certainly not the Japanese language. They are just part of the world's most clunky writing system, and a writing system cannot cause a language to be processed in a different part of the brain any more than it can force it to some other part of the body (excepting, of course, Serbo-Melanesian, which is processed in the left elbow).

George Sansom had the right idea back in the thirties when he noted that the sounds of Japanese,

> simple and few in number, are very well suited to notation by an alphabet, and it is perhaps one of the tragedies of Oriental history that the Japanese genius did not a thousand years ago rise to its invention. Certainly when one considers the truly appalling system which in the course of the centuries they did evolve, that immense and intricate apparatus of signs for recording a few dozen little syllables, one is inclined to think that the western alphabet is perhaps the greatest triumph of the human mind.[1]

To this, I can only add that banana skins provide one of the best surfaces for writing kanji if one is using a ballpoint pen. Since this book is intended to help with an understanding of the Japanese language, it will have nothing further to say about kanji.

Shiru and *Wakaru*
To Know You Is Not Necessarily to Understand You

Believe it or not, one of the first instructors I had when I was a sincere, impressionable beginning student of Japanese at a great educational institution that shall remain nameless but which is situated very close to the shores of Lake Michigan in a very windy city, once told me that the reason the Japanese say *shitte iru* rather than *shiru* for "to know" was to avoid the embarassment of having to say *shirimasu*, containing the *shiri* that means "backside" (in the sense of "butt" or "tush"). Even more amazing than the fact that she told me this was that I BELIEVED HER!

What's that? They told you the same thing?

No, impossible. Any decent textbook will give you the straight dope early on, complete with the information that it's okay to say *shiri* in *shirimasen* when you have to tell someone you don't know something.

Well, if *shirimasen* is okay, why not *shirimasu*?

Obviously, there is something more going on here than delicate avoidance of an anatomical feature—especially among the Japanese, who are far less delicate than we are in discussing physical matters.

The fact is that *shiru* does not mean "to know." It means "to come to know"—"to find out," "to learn."

As the Japanese conceive it, "knowing" consists of finding out about something and keeping it in your brain. When you want to say "I know" in Japanese, you have to say "I have found out about that and I still have it up here where it belongs," or, "I am in a state of having found out."

Shitte iru is very common, but you won't hear *shiru* being used very often in conversation. Unless you realize

94

that *shiru* doesn't mean "to know," however, it could seem stranger than it actually is when you encounter it, as more often happens, in written material. Thus, when Nakamura Mitsuo tells us that the Japanese *mazu gaikei no mohō ni yotte kagaku o shiri* [blush] etc., he is saying they first *learned about* science through the imitation of external forms, not that they *knew* science—and certainly not in the biblical sense.

When you want to say "I don't know" in Japanese, you need to say "I haven't found out about it yet" (*shirimasen*) rather than "I am not in a state of having found out about it" (*shitte imasen*), which, if you could get away with it, would sound more like a declaration of ignorance to be maintained: "I intend to remain in a state of not having found out about it," and although this may, in fact, reflect your own personal conviction, it would sound very strange.

Aside from these problems of meaning and form, *shiru* is not too mysterious. It is transitive, taking direct objects the same way that "know" does in English: *Ano hito o shitte imasu ka* / "Do you know him?" For speakers of English, however, *wakaru* is much trickier.

Wakaru, when it causes trouble, does so through a combination of back-translation and misunderstanding of *wa*. Because "understand" is a transitive verb in English ("I understand that"), students tend to think of *wakaru* as a verb that people do to things (*Watashi wa sore o wakaru*: wrong). Under ordinary circumstances, *wakaru* does not take an *o*-object. People don't *wakaru* things; things themselves do *wakaru*: they "are clear" or they "are understandable," and if we happen to be in the neighborhood, they are clear to us. Notice I said *to* us. If we are going to put people into a sentence about things being clear, they are usually followed by *ni*, as in *Watashi ni wa wakaranai*. When the people in the sentence are *not* followed by *ni*, you should think of this as a kind of contraction: *Watashi wa wakaranai* is short for *Watashi ni wa wakaranai* / "To me, it is not clear."

The trouble probably starts with those contracted forms. *Watashi wa wakaranai* looks awfully close to the transitive English "I don't understand (it)." If you've read "*Wa* and *Ga*: The Answers to Unasked Questions," however, you realize that a *wa*-topic is never the subject of a verb. And if you've read the paragraph before this one, you know that *people* don't do *wakaru*: things do it themselves, so for that reason, too, *watashi* can't be the subject of *wakaru*. Kenkyusha gives us *Share ga wakaru* as "to see [i.e., understand, or get] a joke" and *Share ga wakaranai* as "miss the point of a joke." In both cases, you are saying that the joke itself (subject marked by *ga*) *wakaru*'s or doesn't *wakaru*. If we put "me" into the latter sentence, we get a form that looks like this:

*Watashi **ni wa** sono share **ga** wakaranai.*

Let this be our model for a "full" expression in which the understander and the understandee are both named in a sentence using *wakaru*. A natural English version of this model would be "I don't get that joke," but of course it is a good translation only because it avoids any attempt to reflect the Japanese structure, which is something like "To me, that joke doesn't clarify itself." Perhaps better would be: "That joke doesn't make sense to me."

So you think, Hey, that's easy! The subject of *wakaru* is going to be marked by *ga*! No problem!

Uh, not so fast. Sometimes it'll be *ga* but often it'll be *wa*, too.

And this brings us to another source of vagueness regarding *wakaru*. It seems to be drowning in *wa*'s: sometimes the understander is marked by a *wa*, and sometimes the thing the person is understanding or not understanding is marked with a *wa* instead of a nice, clean *ga*. Let's look at some of the examples from Kenkyusha's long definition of *wakaru*.

Kimi ni wa koko no imi ga wakaru ka / "Can you make out the meaning of this passage?" This corresponds to our "full" model and should be no problem—unless you're not friends with the speaker, who is being far from polite.

Watashi no iu koto ga wakarimasu ka / "Do you understand what I'm saying?" Here, the "you" is understood from context, but otherwise we're still with the model.

Sonna koto wa watashi ni wa chinpun-kanpun de wakaranai / "It's all Greek to me." Here, the "to me" looks familiar, but the "matter" that we are not understanding is marked by *wa* and comes at the beginning of the sentence. If you've read "*Wa* and *Ga*" and "The Myth of the Subjectless Sentence," though, this shouldn't be much of a problem. "As for matters such as that: to me, they [zero pronoun: actual subject] are nonsense and un-understandable."

Kimi no iu imi wa wakatte iru / "I know what you mean." "As far as the meaning of what you're saying goes, it [zero pronoun] is in a state of having become clear." (More on *wakatte iru* later.)

Kare ni wa sono share wa wakaranakatta / "The joke was lost upon him." Wait a minute, here's the same dictionary that gave us *share **ga** wakaranai* now suggesting *share **wa** wakaranai*. Why can't they be more consistent? Actually, with a negative verb like this, *wa* would be more common than the *ga* of the model sentence, merely because *in* a negative sentence you usually want to throw the emphasis ahead to the negative verb. With *wa*, it's more

"He *didn't* get it." With *ga*, it's more "He didn't get it."

Sore o wakaraseru koto ga dekinakatta / "I could not get it across to them." This might look like an *o*-object with *wakaru*, but with the causative, you're causing somebody to act upon something. Plain vanilla *wakaru* does not take objects—except (there's always an exception), as Makino and Tsutsui point out, "when 'non-spontaneous comprehension' is involved . . . in which the experiencer makes a conscious effort to understand something," e.g., *Jakku wa Rinda no kimochi o wakarō to shinai* / "Jack does not try to understand Linda's feelings."

And finally a word on permutations: *wakaru, wakatta, wakatte iru*: "It is clear," "It has (just) become clear," and "It is in a state of having become clear (some time ago)." In English, we might say for these, respectively, "I understand," "Oh, *now* I understand!" and "Alright already!" *Wakatte iru* is a way of shutting someone up: "Look, that was clear to me long before you opened your mouth" = "I know." Of course, if you politen it up, *wakatte imasu*, it's a bit softer. *Wakarimashita* tells people you are understanding what they are now telling you. "Is it clear? Yes, it's clear." *Wakarimashita* denotes instantaneous understanding of something you hadn't seen before: "I see!"

If you read Makino and Tsutsui's neat little article on *wakaru*, meaning "the [spontaneous] process of figuring something out," in contrast to *shiru*, meaning "to get some raw information from some outside source," you, too, will doubtless find yourself saying, *Aa, wakarimashita*![1] This is another instance in which English tends to fudge distinctions that Japanese keeps clear. We say "I know," both when we mean "I comprehend that concept" and when we mean "I am aware of that fact." So the answer to "What are you going to do tonight?" is "I don't know yet," meaning "I haven't figured it out yet"/ *Mada wakarimasen*, no

"I have not come to know that fact yet" / *Mada shiri-masen.* JSL 1:10:280-81 also offers some enlightening analyses and the useful contrasting pair:

> *Tanaka-san o shitte imasu ka* / "Do you know Mr./s. Tanaka?"
> *Michi ga wakarimasu ka* / "Do you know the way?"

Taming *Tame*

The word *tame* can be confusing because it seems to have two entirely different—in fact, virtually opposite—meanings. Sometimes it seems to mean "because so-and-so happened," and at others it seems to mean "in order to make so-and-so happen," which is sort of close to "for the sake of," another common interpretation. How can we tell the difference? By far, the easiest way is to ask the author. Failing that, we are left with our old friend, G. D. Context. One clue that will *not* work is the presence or absence of *ni* after the *tame*. Either kind of *tame* can have a *ni* after it, so don't expect a mechanical approach to work. Look at these pairs:

> *Shiken no tame (ni) benkyō shita* / "I studied for the exam."
> *Shiken no tame (ni) ikenakunatta* / "Because of the exam, I couldn't go."

*

> *Sakana o taberu tame ni tsuri o shite iru* / "He is fishing in order to eat fish."

Sakana o tabeta tame ni tsuri o shite iru / "He is fish
ing because he ate the fish."

Tame means "because" or "owing to" when it follows
a structure implying a completed action or unalterable
state; it means "for the purpose of" when it follows a
structure implying an incomplete (i.e., future) action. Notice that, even though both of the sentences about exams
describe past events, the exam was still a future event in
the first case: the studying was done *for* the upcoming
exam. Likewise, the eating of the fish has yet to occur in
the first sentence about fishing: he is fishing *for the sake of*
being able to eat a fish. In the second exam sentence, the
exam itself may not have taken place when the person became incapable of going (on the picnic, say), but it was an
unalterable fact that *caused* him to become unable to go.
In the second fishing sentence, the fisherman seems to
have given in to his temptations and eaten an earlier-
caught fish, so now he has to replace it with a new one
because of that.

In defending the use of kanji against left-wing critics
who want to get rid of them, Funahashi Seiichi says, "Yes,
it's true that there was a high-pressure selling of the kanji
for 'loyalty' and 'filial piety' [*chū-kō*] in prewar education,"
but, he goes on, *Shikashi, sono **tame** no kanji no haishi
wa, mubō na shōdo-senjutsu ni suginai* / "But getting rid
of kanji *because of that* is sheer overkill," and he continues, *Chūkō sono ta, ichibu no kanji no haishi no **tame** ni,
zen-kanji teppai-ron ni naru koto wa, gyokuseki-konkō de,
issai no kako to no danzetsu de aru* / "Advocating the dis-
carding of all kanji *in order to* get rid of just a few such as
chū and *kō* is to confuse jewels with stones and represents
a complete break with the past."[1] The same author using
the same *tame* in the same paragraph is using it in its two

"opposite" senses. The first, *sono tame*, refers to an accomplished fact in the past, the prewar high-pressure selling of the suspect kanji. The *haishi* of the second occurrence hasn't taken place yet, so *haishi no tame* means "for the sake of getting rid of" or "in order to get rid of." *Haishi no tame* could just as easily mean "because they got rid of" in a context that made it clear that the "getting rid of" was something that had already been done.

Tame, then, signals *purpose* for future actions and *cause* for past actions or unalterably established facts. (Or was it *cause* for future actions and *purpose* for past actions or unalterably established facts? *Future* for actions that have been *cause* on *purpose*, and *past* actions for future facts that have been *altered* to protect the *establishment*? You get the point.)

Tsumori and the Vanishing Beefsteak

Edward Seidensticker is such a magnificent translator of Japanese fiction that I can probably be forgiven for gloating over catching him out at a little flub he made in what happens to be one of his best translations, that of my favorite Kawabata Yasunari novel, *The Sound of the Mountain*. All in the interest of pedagogical accuracy, of course.

The error occurs in one of the key scenes of the book, the moving night passage in Chapter 2, when the aging protagonist hears the mysterious "sound of the mountain" that seems to augur his approaching death. It goes like this in English:

Then he heard the sound of the mountain.

It was a windless night. . . . Not a leaf on the fern by the veranda was stirring. . . . Shingo wondered if he might have heard the sound of the sea. But no—it was the mountain. . . . Thinking that it might be in himself, a ringing in his ears, Shingo shook his head.

The sound stopped, and he was suddenly afraid. A chill passed over him, as if he had been notified that death was approaching. He wanted to question himself, calmly and deliberately, to ask whether it had been the sound of the wind, the sound of the sea, or a sound in his ears. But he had heard no such sound, he was sure. He had heard the mountain.[1]

We might wonder why Shingo "wanted to question himself" about the three possible sources of the sound, since he has just done exactly that. Something is wrong. The Japanese original says, *Kaze no oto ka, umi no oto ka, miminari ka to, Shingo wa reisei ni kangaeta **tsumori** datta ga,*[2] which might better be translated, "Shingo felt certain that he had questioned himself" etc. or "believed (or knew) that he had questioned himself."

As I said, it's just a little flub, and it doesn't materially change the impact of the passage. The culprit here is a usage of *tsumori* that never seems to get explained quite right. Most of the textbooks introduce the word as following non-past verbs with the meaning of "intention": *Ashita iku tsumori desu* / "I intend to go tomorrow." They rarely go on to discuss the use of *tsumori* after perfective verbs, where we see that the word means something more like "belief" or "mind-set" than intention. Makino and Tsutsui give a good example: *Yoku yonda tsumori desu* / "I'm convinced that I read it carefully."[3] "I am of the *tsumori* that I read it carefully [no matter what you may say]."

Of course, someone less fully convinced of his own accuracy might say *Yoku yonda tsumori deshita* / "I *was*
convinced I had read it carefully [until you showed me my
mistake]." Alfonso says, "The basic sense of *tsumori* can
be considered to be 'conviction,' that is, a state of mind
free from doubt,"[4] but doubts can of course be inserted af-
terward. In a *-ta tsumori* construction, one is often defending one's convictions in the face of evidence to the
contrary (a situation that can call forth humor, as we shall
see).

Kenkyusha is extremely generous in offering definitions
that illustrate the broad range of meanings that *tsumori*
can encompass, but it gives only the most inscrutable, tantalizing hint concerning *tsumori* with the perfective, and
that in the form of a kanji compound, *tsumori-chōkin*,
which they translate, using none of their definitions, as
"self-denial savings." This translation can only be understood if you realize that it is possible to say something in
Japanese like this: *Bifuteki o tabeta tsumori de kane o
ginkō ni azuketa* / "I put my money in the bank with the
tsumori that I had eaten a steak." Well, where's the steak?
It has vanished. Or rather, it never existed. I denied myself
the steak, told myself that I was being good and doing the
right thing by saving my money instead. I mentally enjoyed
the imaginary steak to compensate for the unexciting act of
handing my money over to the teller. Sigh. A few more
examples:

> *Mō yatchatta tsumori da kedo.* / "I assume I already
> did it all, but . . . [am I wrong?]"[5]
> *Isshōkenmei yatta tsumori desu.* / "I believe I did
> my best."[6]
> *Shinda tsumori ni nareba donna koto de mo dekiru.* /
> "If you tell yourself 'I have died' [Oh, well, the

worst thing that can happen to me is I'll get killed],
you can do anything."[7]

Perhaps I ought to add that it's not so much the mechanical combination of *-ta + tsumori* that does the job as
the use of *tsumori* after something that implies an ongoing
condition or accomplished fact rather than futurity. A
noun-*no-tsumori* or adjective + *tsumori* can work just as
well:

Ano ko wa mō otona no tsumori desu ne. / "That kid
thinks he's a grownup already, eh?"[8]
Ano ojiisan wa mada wakai tsumori nan desu yo. /
"That old man considers himself still young."[9]

Given the right situation, *tsumori* can be a source of
ironic or self-deprecating humor. A lively lady brought
some homemade sweet bean pastries (*manjū*) to a party at
my house earlier tonight and was asked by a wry gentle-
man, *Manjū desu ka* / "Are those manjū?" He obviously
knew what they were but was gently kidding her about
their slightly unorthodox appearance. Without batting an
eyelash, she answered, *Manjū no tsumori desu kedo* /
"Well, in my humble opinion they are manjū." She got a
good laugh, and you can, too, next time someone asks you
something that is fairly obvious:

Amerika no kata desu ka / "Are you an American?"
*Amerika-jin no **tsumori** desu kedo . . .* / "Well, I was
the last time I looked. . . ."

Here, for extra credit, is a wonderful, long sentence
using *tsumori* from an interview with the novelist Murakami Haruki, in which he denies that he ever consciously

sought to be at the forefront of a new "urbanization" movement in literature: *Boku wa kesshite sō iu mono o motomete ita wake de mo nai shi, ima de mo motomete nai shi, jibun no kakitai koto o jibun no kakitai yō ni kaku to iu itten ni ishiki o shūchū shite yatte kita **tsumori** nan desu keredo ne* / "I never was striving for anything like that and I am not striving for it now; I *believe* that what I have done all along is to concentrate my attention on one point, and that is to write about what I want to write about in the way I want to write about it."[10]

You Say *Kimeru* and I Say *Kimaru*

Keeping this particlar transitive/intransitive pair straight can be more difficult than you'd imagine. See if this scheme helps:

> *X o kimeru*: to pick a category (*Heya o kimeta* / "We decided on *a* room").
> *X ga kimaru*: a category gets picked (*Heya ga kimatta* / "A room has been decided on").

*

> *X ni kimeru*: to pick an individual (*Kono heya ni kimeta* / "We decided on this room").
> *X ni kimaru*: an individual gets picked (*Kono heya ni kimatta* / "This room turned out to be the one").

Warning
This Language Works Backwards

As usual, official policies of the United States toward Japan are totally misdirected. Instead of pressuring the Japanese into lowering trade barriers or taking a greater share of the responsibility for their own defense, we should be urging them to bring their verbs from the ends of their sentences into second place, right after their subjects, where they belong. Unless we accomplish this, the rest of our foreign policy is so much tofu.

If you think you have trouble with Japanese verbs being withheld from you until you get through all the intervening time expressions and modifying clauses and whatever else the writer decides to put in your way, don't worry: the Japanese have the same problem themselves. They know their language works backwards, but they persist in keeping it that way as a matter of national pride.

Of course, some writers, such as Kabuki playwrights, have capitalized on the perverse placement of the verb at the end. The theater is charged with suspense as the retainer, center stage, slowly, tantalizingly intones the lines, "As to the question . . . of whether or not this severed head . . . is the head of my liege lord, the mighty general Kajimura Saburō Mitsumaru . . . known throughout the land for his brilliant military escapades . . . beloved by the people of his domain for his benevolence towards even the lowliest farmer . . . I can say, here and now, without a single doubt clouding my mind . . . that although the throngs gathered here before us may wish the truth to be otherwise . . . and the happiness of his entire family hangs in the balance . . . this my master's head . . . is . . . NOT!" More often, though, instead of enjoying the delicious dilemma of

106

having to wait to the end, users of Japanese give each other and expect to be given little hints along the way of what lies in store for them.

Take conditional expressions, for example. In English, we know we're getting a conditional right from the start: "If you buy it today, you can save fifty percent." Since most Japanese don't want the unpleasant surprise of finding a *ba* or *tara* ("if") ending attached to a verb they expected to be a straightforward statement, they'll flash each other the adverb *moshi*, which we also translate "if," early in the sentence, often at the very beginning. Kenkyusha gives us, **Moshi** *tenki ga yokat***tara** *ashita undō-kai ga aru* / "If the weather's good, tomorrow there will be an athletic meet." We don't translate the *moshi* and the *tara* separately; they work together as a pair, which we represent as a single "if."

Japanese has lots of other such pairs consisting first of an early-warning element and second the construction that does the actual work, usually as an inflection of the verb or some other expression associated with the verb and therefore held off until a later point in the sentence. Like *moshi* and *ba*, they work together and do not call for separate translation. The following are some examples.

Maru-de is an adverb meaning "entirely" that often warns you a comparison is coming, as in **Maru-de** *shachō* **mitai** *ni mieru* / "He looks as if he were the president of the company" and **Maru-de** *kichigai no yō da* / "He looks as if he's mad" (both from Kenkyusha). We could throw in a "just" for the *maru-de*, but it isn't necessary. **Maru-de** *kōri no ue o subette iru* **mitai** *da* / "It's *just like* skating on ice."[1] **Maru-de** *etsubo o irodoru kin-iro no e-no-gu no* **yō** *ni, taiyō no hikari ga ie-jū ni shitatari-ochite ita* / "The sunlight dripped over the house like golden paint over an art jar."[2]

Expressions such as *naze nara* or *naze ka to iu to* or *dōshite ka to ieba* ("if you ask why") warn you that an explanation is coming, probably with a construction such as *kara da* ("it's because") at the end. For example, Takahashi Kazumi tells us it would be useless to look for the key to a novel in the facts of the writer's life, and then he remarks, **Naze ka to iu to** *'jijitsu' to iu mono wa, shōsetsu-ka ga naizai sasete iru kattō no inshi o shigeki shi, sōzō to shikō no undō o okosaseru koto wa dekite mo, sono kattō no kōzu sono mono o keisei suru koto mo hen'yū suru koto mo dekinai* **kara de aru** / *"The reason for this is that* while 'facts' may be able to stimulate the elements of turmoil that the writer has within himself and set his imaginative and thought processes in motion, they are incapable of either forming or transforming the composition of the turmoil itself."[3] See the *kara da* section of "The Explainers" for several more examples.

Tada, an adverb, and *dake*, a postposition, both of which can work independently and which are usually translated "just" or "only," often work in pairs, with the *tada* warning you that the *dake* is coming. **Tada** *ironna koto ga sono jiken o sakai ni yukkuri to henka shite itta* **dake** *sa* / *"It's just* that all kinds of things gradually started to change after that incident."[4] One "just" will do for the pair.

A much heavier-sounding version of *tada . . . dake* is *hitasura . . . nomi. Hitasura*, an adverb meaning "intently," and, by extension, "concentrating solely upon" or just "solely," turns out to be nothing more than a fancy written-style version of *tada,* likewise anticipating *dake* (or *nomi,* a written-style *dake*), as in Kenkyusha's *Kanojo wa* **hitasura** *naku* **nomi** *de atta* / *"She did nothing but* cry." **Hitasura** *Nihon-jin* **dake** *wa risuku o sake, kiken kara tōzakatte itai* / *"The Japanese want to be the only* ones who avoid all the risks and keep a distance between themselves and danger."[5]

The rest of the examples are of this latter sort: more literary in nature and less commonly heard in speech.

Tatoe (*tatoi*) is an adverb meaning "even if" or "even supposing" that warns you that you are going to get a *-te* (*-de*) *mo*, which also means "even if" or "even supposing," as in *Kare wa sonna tokoro e **tatoe** iku koto ga atte **mo** goku mare da* / "*Even if* he does go to such places, it's very seldom" (Kenkyusha). ***Tatoi** dōtoku-teki hihan o kudasu beki bunshi ga konnyū shite kuru jiken ni tsui**temo** kore o tokugi-teki ni kaishaku shinai de, tokugi to wa maru-de kankei no nai kokkei to nomi miru koto mo dekiru* / "*Even supposing* it is in regard to an event into which some small element deserving moral censure becomes commingled, we can choose not to interpret this ethically but to view it as entirely comical and having nothing to do with ethics."[6]

Aruiwa, an adverb meaning "maybe" or "perhaps," anticipates an expression of the same meaning, *ka mo shirenai*, as in ***Aruiwa** sō **ka mo shirenai*** / "It might be so." *Sakura no mori no mankai no himitsu wa dare ni mo ima mo wakarimasen. **Aruiwa** 'kodoku' to iu mono de atta **ka mo shirenai*** / "Even now, no one knows the secret of the cherry forest in full bloom. *Perhaps* it was what we call 'solitude.'"[7]

Iyashikumo ("even a little") . . . *ijō* (or *kara ni wa*) is a pair that, together, means "insofar as so-and-so is the case" or "as long as you're going to do so-and-so." Kenkyusha and my mother give us ***Iyashikumo** yaru **kara ni wa** yoku yare* / "If you do it at all, do it well," and Kenkyusha ***Iyashikumo** tatakau **kara ni wa** akumade tatakae* / "If you do fight, fight to the finish." *Jidōsha no nai mukashi wa iza-shirazu, **iyashikumo** hatsumei sareru **ijō** jinrikisha wa jidōsha ni makenakereba naranai* /

"Leaving aside the question of the old days before the automobile existed, *now that it **has** been* invented, the rickshaw will inevitably give way to the automobile."[8]

In general, these early warnings, which give aid and comfort to English speakers, are more characteristic of written than spoken Japanese. When Japanese people speak English, though, you sometimes hear them making sentences that work much like these matched pairs. They'll start out with normal English thought order, "Maybe so-and-so," but toward the end of the sentence they instinctively feel the need for inserting the "maybe" again where it "belongs," so you hear, "Maybe they couldn't make it, maybe," or "I think I'll go now, I think." Please don't do that when *you* are translating such pairs from Japanese.

The Pleasures of Reading Japanese

I often warn my literature students, especially those whose language skills have reached the stage where they can handle new texts with some degree of independence, that, as they read, they should try to maintain a distinction between literary pleasure afforded by the work itself and what might be called "linguistic pleasure" stimulated by the sheer satisfaction of making their way successfully through an orthographical garden, the gathering of whose fruits is only becoming possible for them after years of disciplined study. For the fact is that Japanese, especially for those of us who have learned to read it after childhood, never loses its exotic appeal; each page turned reveals to the eye a new spectacle of outlandish squiggles that momentarily takes the breath away. And written in those squiggles or spoken by the people who were raised in the language are equally outlandish syntactic structures—not only passives but causatives and passive-causatives and *te*-forms with *oku*'s attached or *morau*'s and *itadaku*'s and *zu*'s that make our minds work in ways that can never be conveyed to those who do not know the language. There is a thrill in realizing that you can process this stuff with your very own brain.

I have long been convinced that, as we speak—but especially as we read this foreign tongue—just beneath the threshold of consciousness, a voice continually shouts, "Look, Mom, I'm reading Japanese!" And these subliminal cries arouse in us a pleasure that can easily be confused with the satisfaction of reading a good story or book. In fact, there is a danger that the simpler the style of a work and the less challenging its content (which is to say, the easier a piece of writing is to "understand" on the purely lexical level) the more likely it is to grant us that instant gratification of having read something of exceptional interest.

For years, I assumed that this was a handicap unique to the foreign reader of Japanese literature. Some months ago, however, at the request of a scholarly journal, I translated an essay on contemporary economic problems that had all too obviously been ground out in response to the insatiable needs of Japan's publishing industry. The more I struggled to find English equivalents for its journalistic hyperboles, its catchy neologisms intended to startle and stun, the more convinced I became that the Japanese read their own language the same way we do.

The woman who wrote the piece is quite the media figure these days, in demand as much for her ravishing good looks as for her fresh pronouncements on the contemporary scene. I couldn't help feeling that there was an inescapable connection between that and the clever manner in which she combined Chinese characters to manufacture new concepts—or at least concepts that *sounded* new and looked new on the page. Perhaps she has something important to tell her readers, but there can be little doubt from the way she puts her words together that her first intention is to entertain them, to make them feel as if they have just read something new and important. And, having struggled year after year to learn the thousands of characters needed to read and write modern literate Japanese, her readers respond with a thrill of satisfaction, and perhaps with their own subliminal shouts: "I *understand* what this beautiful, brainy woman is telling me! Look, Okaasan, I'm reading Japanese!"

The Unbelievable Complexity of Being
Aru vs. De Aru

Shakespeare posed the problem most memorably and succinctly: "To be, or not to be—that is the question." There can be no doubt about what "to be" means here: certainly not "to be" an onion or "to be" green, but simply "to be," to exist, as in "I think, therefore I am." If Descartes had wanted to use the kind of "to be" meaning "equals," he would have written, "I think, therefore I am René." The "to be" meaning "having the quality of" might have yielded "I think, therefore I am cool." Let's face it, English is a hopelessly vague language which fails to make even the simplest distinctions.

Not Japanese, however. It ignores the picky difference between "equals-be" and "having the quality-be," but it has two different kinds of "to be," the "equals" type and the "exists" type, and it keeps them completely separate. This is such a fundamental feature of the language that carelessness in this area can—and far too often does—lead to major misunderstandings.

Now, wouldn't it be nice if we could say that one type of "to be" in Japanese is *aru* and the other is *orohonpo*: no one would ever get them mixed up. Unfortunately, one is *aru* and the other one often takes the form *de aru*, the written equivalent of the spoken *da* or *desu*, and non-Japanese get them mixed up all the time. To make matters worse, the *de* and the *aru* can be split up within a sentence. Most of the time, this is done by a *wa*, so as to put more emphasis on the positive *aru*:

> *Watashi wa neko de aru.* / "I am a cat."
> *Watashi wa neko de wa aru ga . . .* / "I *am* a cat, but
> . . . (that doesn't mean I like to eat mice)."

The most widely separated *de* and *aru* I have seen occurs in the novella *Ku no sekai* (World of Pain) by Uno Kōji after the hero's common-law wife accuses him of being a dweeb and he reflects: *Ikujinashi! Soshite mattaku sono tōri **de** watashi wa **atta** no da* / "A dweeb! Yes, I was that—exactly!"[1]

The distinction between the two kinds of "being" is an old one, and it shows up in the famous poem by the Heian poet Narihira, in which *nai*, the modern negative of *aru*, appears as *aranu*, and instead of modern *de wa nai* we find *naranu*:

> *Tsuki ya **aranu***   Is there not the moon?

Haru ya mukashi no	And *is not* the spring
Haru naranu	The spring of old?
Waga mi hitotsu wa	My self alone
Moto no mi ni shite	Remaining as it was . . .

The implication being that if everything is the way it was in the old days, why isn't my mistress here any more? Much of the wild variation among English translations of this poem has to do with the degree of the translators' fidelity to the difference between *aru* and *de aru* (ancient *ari* and *nari*).

The poem illustrates, too, that the difference between "exist-be" and "equals-be" applies to the negative forms as well, the negatives of *aru* and *de aru* being *nai* and *de wa* (or *ja*) *nai*.

Here's a useful pair to keep in mind: *nanimo nai* and *nandemo nai*.

The first one means "There isn't anything," "We have nothing," etc. The second one means "It's nothing." Thus, *nanimo nai tokoro* is a place where there exists nothing: they don't have any furniture or entertainment or anything. *Nandemo nai tokoro* is a nothing place, a place that's nothing at all, a worthless, boring dump.

Somewhat less problematical than the distinction between *aru* and *de aru* is that between *aru* and *iru*. Snow shovels and toothpaste tubes *aru*, while people and leopards *iru*. *Pen ga aru* / "There's a pen here," but *Kitabatake-san ga iru* / "Ms. Kitabatake is here." The biggest challenge with this is simply remembering to use *aru* with inanimate and *iru* with animate subjects. Sometimes, though, when speaking of people in the abstract, you can use *aru*: *Otōto ga aru* / "I have a younger brother."

One of the highly un-English things that *iru* does is to act like a volitional verb (the strain of trying to use "to be" this way is what makes the opening of Hamlet's speech startling). When the police take Mume's father away to Sugamo prison and she chooses to stay on the island, she declares tearfully to her teacher, *Sensei, atashi koko ni iru* / "Sensei, I'm going to stay here!" (in the film *Setouchi shōnen yakyūdan* / "MacArthur's Children," 1985).

By the way, *orohonpo* is a real word in the Saga dialect, and it means "I'm not too crazy about it," which is probably how most students feel about having to keep track of *aru* and *de aru*.

Go Jump in the Lake, But Be Sure to Come Back

The idiomatic Japanese way of saying "Go do so-and-so," is "Do so-and-so and come." Instead of "Go jump in the lake," a Japanese would say, "Jump in the lake and come." Such commands should be issued to literal-minded foreigners only in outdoor settings. Native Japanese don't *say* go jump in the lake, so the form poses no inherent danger to your carpet with them. Here, though, are some authentic examples of the form:

> *Yattsukete koi.* / "Go get the bastards!"
> *Sanpo de mo shite atama o hiyashite koyō.* / "I think I'll take a walk and try to cool down."[1]
> *Okane o moratte kite kudasai.* / "Please go get the money."
> *Yasai ni mizu o yatte kite chōdai.* / "Go water the vegetables, will you?"

Fiddlers Three = Three Fiddlers?

Old King Cole called for "his fiddlers three" mainly because they rhymed with "soul was he." If questions of rhyme and meter hadn't entered into the picture, he could just as well have called for "his three fiddlers," who, we know from the "his," were a unit of some sort. If we wanted to keep them as a unit in Japanese, however, we couldn't be quite so indifferent about word order.

Old King Kōroku would have *Sannin no baiorin-hiki o yobiyoseta* rather than *Baiorin-hiki o sannin yobiyoseta.* The second version would mean "He called for three fiddlers," three chosen at random rather than the self-contained string band he was used to.

The normal place to put counters is *after* the noun in question, where it functions as an adverb telling to what extent the verb is to be performed. *Enpitsu o sanbon kudasai* means "Please give me three pencils"—*any* three pencils out of a larger supply. *Sanbon no enpitsu,* with the counter now modifying the noun itself, means "Please give me the three pencils."

Kurosawa's movie about a group of "seven samurai" is called *Shichinin no samurai.* If someone singlehandedly killed that famous group, he would have *Shichinin no samurai o koroshita,* but if, in his wanderings, he happened to kill seven guys who were samurai, he would have *Samurai o shichinin koroshita.*

Itō Sei had far less dramatic doings in mind when he wrote: *Watashi-tachi ikkō shichinin no Nihon-jin wa, asa hayaku Tashikento o ta[tta]* / "Our seven-member Japanese group left Tashkent early in the morning."[1]

Eating in the Wrong Direction

Long, long before you ever heard of directional verbs of giving and receiving and realized that because of its fixed directionality the verb *itadaku* could be used in the kind of complex constructions discussed in the "Invisible Man" chapter, you probably learned it as the polite formula you utter before eating, Japan's answer to saying grace: *Itadaki-masu*, meaning more or less literally, "I humbly receive." (*Literally*, it means to place something on your head or hold something over your head, a gesture intended as a humble expression of awestruck gratitude, but don't do this with your food.)

Then you probably learned *itadaku* as the normal humble verb for eating and drinking, to be used in place of the more neutral *taberu* and *nomu*. You learned, too, that there is an honorific verb, *meshiagaru*, to be used in reference to the eating and drinking of others to whom you are speaking politely. You yourself can never *meshiagaru*, only honored guests and the like can do that when you are speaking to or about them.

If, indeed, you have learned all this, then you would have been just as surprised as I was the other night at a Seattle sushi bar when the young sushi "chef" (*itamae-san*, the man in front of the cutting board), a recent arrival from Japan, politely asked me at the end of the meal, *Orenji itadakimasu ka.*

In his mind, no doubt, this was the "polite" way of asking me whether I wanted to eat an orange for dessert. It was, indeed, "polite," but in the wrong direction: it wasn't honorific toward me but a humble verb that could only properly used to describe his humbly receiving something from his listener. What he was really asking me was,

"Would you like most humbly to receive an orange from my lofty self?" I blinked and smiled and got a sweet, juicy, and cleverly sliced orange in return.

I was tempted to chalk this one up to the increasingly scandalous unfamiliarity of the younger generation with proper modes of speech that one hears and reads complaints about, mostly from the older generation. Then it occurred to me there was something familiar about this, something that went all the way back to the immediate postwar period.

In 1947, Dazai Osamu (then 38) published his novel *Shayō* (The Setting Sun), which was a sensational bestseller and bequeathed its name to a generation of declining aristocrats. Unfortunately for Dazai, one writer who identified strongly with those aristocrats, Mishima Yukio, ridiculed the book for its utterly uninformed portrait of the upper crust. His most damning piece of evidence was Dazai's use of *itadaku* where he should have used *meshiagaru*.[1]

Dazai Osamu was one of the great stylists of modern Japanese fiction, and much of his humor derives from the way he plays with levels of speech and diction. Had he not committed suicide in 1948, he might be 83 today and complaining about the younger generation's ignorance of Japanese.

NOTES

Introduction

1. "Japanese Language," *Funk and Wagnall's New Encyclopedia*, 27 vols. (New York, 1975) 14:158.

2. See Helmut Morsbach, "Words are Not Enough: Reading Between the Lines in Japanese Communication," *Japan Society Newsletter* (New York, March 1989) for both of these views.

3. Irie Takanori, review of *Injurious to Public Morals: Writers and the Meiji State*, by Jay Rubin, in *Japan Quarterly* (October-December, 1984), pp. 459-60, and expanded remarks in *Japan Quarterly* (January-March, 1985), p. 113.

4. Hatanaka Shigeo, quoted in my *Injurious to Public Morals: Writers and the Meiji State* (Seattle: University of Washington Press, 1984), p. 261.

5. See Roy Andrew Miller's *The Japanese Language* (The University of Chicago Press, 1967), pp. ix-x, for a strong dose of common sense.

6. Paul Aoki, Director of the Language Learning Center, University of Washington, has kindly shared these facts and figures with me. The definition of "Limited Working Proficiency" comes from a government document called "Interagency Language Roundtable Language Skill Level Descriptions" (p. 9). This document says nothing about the forty-seven-week recovery program, which is a closely guarded secret.

The Myth of the Subjectless Sentence

1. Okutsu Keiichiro, *"Boku wa unagi da" no bunpō* (Kuroshio Shuppan, 1978).

2. Adapted from Woody Allen, "The Condemned," in *Side Effects* (New York: Ballantine Books, 1981), p. 15.

3. Certain grammarians believe that "he" was originally Sir William Snodgrass of Ramsgate Heather, Surrey.

4. Eleanor Harz Jorden with Mari Noda, *Japanese: The Spoken Language* (JSL), 3 vols. (New Haven and London: Yale University Press, 1987) 1:59.

5. They suddenly acquire this nasty habit in one of the types of text that students most want to read: newspapers.

6. The answer is three: the speaker, the listener, and the person in charge, whom the listener is supposed to make do "it," an action that can be known only from context. In this particular passage, the action called for is putting two single beds together to make a double. From Watanabe Jun'ichi, "*Nihongo de okoru*," *Chūō Kōron* (January 1989), p. 39.

Wa and *Ga*

1. Steve Allen, *The Question Man* (New York: Bellmeadows Press, 1959), pp. 27–28. This rare source also includes A: "He shot down ten Japanese planes." Q: "Why was Suki Yamamoto kicked out of the Japanese Air Force?"
2. "Haritsuke," *Encyclopedia Japonica / Dai Nihon hyakka jiten*, 23 vols. (Shōgakukan, 1967–72) 14:721.
3. Watanabe Jun'ichi, "*Nihongo de okoru*," *Chūō Kōron* (January 1989), p. 39.
4. Murakami Haruki, *Hitsuji o meguru bōken* (Kōdansha Bunko, 1985) 1:182. See the translation by Alfred Birnbaum, *A Wild Sheep Chase* (Tokyo: Kodansha International, 1989), p. 115: "The narcotics eased the pain all right, but they also resulted in hallucinations."
5. I blame my colleague John Treat for this discouraging observation. Neither he nor I believe, however, that the difficulty of *wa* and *ga* is any more than that: a linguistic difficulty, much of which, with proper training and conceptualization, can be overcome. See Alfonso, 2:967–993, for an excellent series of *wa* and *ga* drills. Notice that Alfonso does not attempt the definitive comparison and contrast until his thirty-third lesson, after students have had a great deal of experience with the language, and then he devotes twenty-seven pages to this thorny problem.
6. For another view, see Susumu Kuno, *The Structure of the Japanese Language* (Cambridge: The MIT Press, 1973), pp. 79–95.
7. Anthony Alfonso, *Japanese Language Patterns*, 2 vols. (Tokyo: Sophia University L. L. Center of Applied Linguistics, 1966).
8. "Eli is Home," *Journal American* (June 12, 1989), p. 1.
9. Basil Hall Chamberlain, *A Handbook of Colloquial Japanese*, fourth edition revised (London and Yokohama: Crosby Lockwood and Son and Kelly and Walsh, Ltd., 1907), pp. 85–86. The preface to the fourth edition says (on p. i) that the book is little changed from the earlier editions of 1888, 1889, and 1898. See also W. G. Aston, *A Grammar of the Japanese Written Language*, second edition (London and Yokohama: Trübner & Co. and Lane, Crawford & Co., 1877), p. 132, which suggests such En-

glish parallels for *wa* as "with respect to," "in the case of," "in so far as regards," and "at any rate." Clay MacCauley, *An Introductory Course in Japanese* (Tokyo: Shueisha, 1896), a book far inferior to Chamberlain's for clarity of exposition, gives "as for" and also notes in the preface that the author has "freely used" Chamberlain's *Handbook*. See pp. III, 166–67. Rudolf Lange, *A Text-book of Colloquial Japanese*, English edition by Christopher Noss (Tokyo: Methodist Publishing House, 1903), a generally muddled presentation of Japanese grammar, does distinguish *wa* from *ga* by reference to the questions they answer (p. 3), but the book inexplicably omits any reference to Steve Allen.

10. *Asahi Shinbun* March 12, 1989, p. 17.

11. Of course the *da* here can be viewed not as a copula but as a shortened substitute for *ni suru* or *ga tabetai*, much as "do" can be substituted for longer verbal structures ("Who wants to be the first one on his block to own a Captain Video decoder ring?" "I do."). Since we're dealing with unspoken ideas, it doesn't much matter whether we interpret them as verbs or nouns; personally, I like to treat *da* as a consistent copula, with the context doing the flip-flops. Okutsu Keiichiro sensibly points out that the flexibility of *da* is another feature of Japanese (along with the frequent disappearance of nouns, as discussed in the previous chapter) that prompts people to call it a vague language, but that people communicate just fine using these structures within both verbal and nonverbal contexts. See Okutsu Keiichiro, *"Boku wa unagi da" no bunpō* (Kuroshio Shuppan, 1978), pp. 12–13.

12. Murakami Haruki, *Sekai no owari to hādoboirudo wandārando* (Shinchōsha, 1985; Shincho Bunko, 1988) 1:11.

13. Kunikida Doppo, *"Kawagiri"* (1989); Nakagami Kenji, *"Mizu no onna," Nakagami Kenji zen-tanpen shōsetsu* (Kawada Shobō Shinsha, 1984), p. 630.

The Invisible Man's Family Reunion

1. By contrast, the concept of original sin helps explain the Western fixation on who did what, when, with whom, and using which paraphernalia.

2. Beware the note on *morau* in John Young and Kimiko Nakajima-Okano, *Learn Japanese*, 4 vols. (Honolulu: University of Hawaii Press, 1984), 1:181, which glosses the word as "get or receive (something from someone)" or "is given."

3. *"Nihongo de okuru," Chūō Kōron* (January 1989), p. 39.

4. Hoshi Shin'ichi, *"Kata no ue no hisho,"* in *Akuma no iru ten-*

goku (Hayakawa Bunko JA9: Hayakawa Shobō, 1973), p. 104. Actually, the speaker is not the salesman himself but his robot parrot. I am not making this up.

5. One other possible interpretation of *Kaban o nusumareta* is that the passive is being used for purely honorific purposes: "He most exaltedly stole the suitcase." I am not discussing here the use of passives and passive-causatives for mere politeness, in which the rule of thumb is the more syllables, the politer. If the Emperor stole the suitcase, you could have *Tennō-heika ni okaseraremashite wa kaban o o-nusumi ni naraseraremashita*, in which a mere one-syllable *wa* is stretched to ten syllables. Usually, the context will tell you that the writer is using the passive for honorific purposes.

6. Murakami Haruki, *"Tonii Takitani," Murakami Haruki zen-sakuhin 1979–1989*, 8 vols. (Kōdansha, 1991) 8:227.

7. JSL 1:323. Diacritics omitted here.

8. Thanks to Michio Tsutsui for bringing this to my attention.

9. See "The Explainers" for a discussion of the *kara* at the end.

10. Alfonso, *Japanese Language Patterns* 2:952.

11. Murakami Haruki, *"Hito-kui neko," Murakami Haruki zen-sakuhin* 8:270.

The Explainers

1. Don't confuse this with a *kara da* following a verb in the -*te* from, which will mean "It was *after* so-and-so," not *because*. Be sure you understand the difference between *Itta kara* and *Itte kara*. This footnote looks like a conveniently obscure place for me to mention that I have no explanation for the whereabouts of the zero pronoun when the copula disappears as well: *Hayaku neru. Nemui kara*.

2. Murakami Haruki, *"Zō no shōmetsu,"* in *Murakami Haruki zen-sakuhin 1979–1989*, 8 vols. (Kōdansha, 1991), 8:40.

3. Mishima Yukio, *"Watakushi no henreki jidai," Mishima Yukio bungaku ronshū* (Kōdansha, 1970), p. 322. Again the translation conflates *Naze nara* and *kara de aru*. For an interpretation of *kangaerareru*, see "The Invisible Man's Family Reunion: The Natural Potential."

4. Mishima, op. cit., p. 307. I have omitted the parenthetical comment, *sono naka no jibun no zenbu ga sō da to wa iwanai ga r* "I'm not saying that the whole of me in it is that way, but," an unnecessary complication here.

5. Howard Hibbett and Gen Itasaka, *Modern Japanese: A Basic*

Reader, 2 vols. (Cambridge: Harvard University Press, 1967) 2:23.

6. *Japanese Language Patterns* 1:405.

7. Murakami Haruki, "*Midori-iro no kemono*," *Bungakukai* Special April Issue (April 1991), p. 30.

8. Murakami, op. cit., pp. 40–41.

The Johnny Carson *Hodo*

1. These examples have been taken from alert journalist Dave Barry's column in the *Seattle Times* (July 22, 1991), p. A-6, and do not necessarily represent the opinions of Johnny Carson, Ed McMahon, the NBC television network, or anyone else for that matter, including Dave Barry.

2. See Alfonso 2:700 ff. for a full comparison. Occasionally the kanji compound *teido* is used.

3. Examples from Alfonso 703, Kenkyusha: *hodo* 1:2, Mikino and Tsutsui 136, etc.

Kanji

1. G. B. Sansom, *Japan: A Short Cultural History* (New York: Appleton-Century-Crofts, Inc., 1931, 1943), p. 136.

Shiru and *Wakaru*

1. Makino and Tsutsui, pp. 529–31.

Taming *Tame*

1. In "*Kokugo mondai to minzoku no shōrai*," *Chūō Kōron* (May, 1961), pp. 48–56.

Tsumori and the Vanishing Beefsteak

1. Yasunari Kawabata, *The Sound of the Mountain*, tr. Edward G. Seidensticker (New York: Knopf, 1970), p. 8.

2. *Kawabata Yasunari zenshū*, 14 vols. (Shinchōsha, 1969) 8:234.

3. P. 504.

4. Alfonso, *Japanese Language Patterns* 2:860.

5. JSL 2:20:203.

6. Alfonso 2:859, but poorly translated there as "I intended to do my best."

7. From Kenkyusha, under *shinu*, p. 1,564, which translates the sentence, "Nothing is impossible to one who does not fear death."

8. Alfonso 2:859, translation slightly altered.

9. Alfonso 2:861.

10. Kawamoto Saburo, "'*Monogatari*' *no tame no bōken: Murakami Haruki*," *Bungakukai* (August 1985), p. 40.

Warning

1. Murakami Haruki, "*Nemuri*," *Bungakukai* (January 1989), p. 46.

2. F. Scott Fitzgerald, "The Ice Palace," tr. Murakami Haruki, *Mai rosuto shitii* (Chūko Bunko, 1981), p. 81.

3. "*Bonnō-suru mi toshite*," in Mainichi Shinbunsha Gakugei-bu, ed., *Watakushi no shōsetsu sahō* (Sekkasha, 1966), p. 210.

4. Murakami Haruki, "*Pan'ya sai-shugeki*," *Pan'ya sai-shugeki* (Bunshun Bunko, 1989), p. 21.

5. Ito Ken'ichi, "The Japanese State of Mind: Deliberations on the Gulf Crisis," *Journal of Japanese Studies* 17:2 (Summer 1991), p. 281.

6. Natsume Sōseki, "*Bungei to dōtoku*," SZ 11:378:11. Sōseki is speaking in this ponderous language about the moral dilemma created by a lecturer who farts loudly before his audience.

7. Sakaguchi Ango, "*Sakura no mori no mankai no shita*," *Gendai Nihon bungaku zenshū*, 100 vols. (Chikuma Shobō, 1967), p. 166.

8. Natsume Sōseki, "*Gendai Nihon no kaika*," SZ 11:332.

The Unbelievable Complexity of Being

1. In *Nihon gendai bungaku zenshū* (Kōdansha, 1964) 58:233. I use "dweeb" here in the sense of "gutless wonder" rather than as the precise equivalent of "dork."

Go Jump in the Lake, But Be Sure to Come Back

1. Jeffrey G. Garrison, "*Body*" *Language* (Tokyo: Kodansha International, 1990), p. 17.

Fiddlers Three = Three Fiddlers?

1. Itō Sei, "*Bibihanun e no seppun*," *Itō Sei zenshū*, vols. (Shinchōsha, 1974), 12:444.

Eating in the Wrong Direction

1. Mishima Yukio, "*Watakushi no henreki jidai*," in *Mishima Yukio bungaku-ron shū* (Kōdansha, 1970), p. 315.

KODANSHA'S COMPACT KANJI GUIDE

A compact Japanese-English character dictionary based on the 1,945 *Jōyō* ("common use") *Kanji*. Includes 20,000 practical words.

ISBN 4-7700-1553-4; vinyl flexibinding; 928 pages

THE COMPLETE GUIDE TO EVERYDAY KANJI

Yaeko S. Habein and Gerald B. Mathias

A systematic guide to remembering and understanding the 1,945 *Jōyō* ("common use") *Kanji*.

ISBN 0-87011-793-9; paperback; 344 pages

LET'S LEARN HIRAGANA
ISBN 0-87011-709-2; paperback; 72 pages

LET'S LEARN KATAKANA
ISBN 0-87011-719-X; paperback; 88 pages

Yasuko Kosaka Mitamura

These workbooks explain in simple, clear steps how to read and write *hiragana* and *katakana*.

JAPANESE KANA WORKBOOK

P. G. O'Neill

Designed to give the beginning student a systematic introduction to the *kana* and their usage.
ISBN 0-87011-039-X; paperback; 128 pages

POWER JAPANESE SERIES